THE

PUBLICATIONS

OF THE

SURTEES SOCIETY

VOL. 205

Edmund Tew. Courtesy of Christ's Hospital

THE

PUBLICATIONS

OF THE

SURTEES SOCIETY

ESTABLISHED IN THE YEAR
M.DCCC.XXXIV

ISSN: 0307–5362

VOL. CCV

At a MEETING of the SURTEES SOCIETY, held on June 10 1999, it was ORDERED —
'That the Justicing Notebook (1750–64) of Edmund Tew, Rector of Boldon, edited by Dr Gwenda Morgan and Dr Peter Rushton, should be printed as a volume of the Society's publications'

THE JUSTICING NOTEBOOK (1750–64) OF EDMUND TEW, RECTOR OF BOLDON

EDITED AND WITH AN INTRODUCTION

BY

GWENDA MORGAN AND
PETER RUSHTON

THE SURTEES SOCIETY

THE BOYDELL PRESS

First published 2000

A Surtees Society Publication
published by The Boydell Press
an imprint of Boydell & Brewer Ltd
PO Box 9, Woodbridge, Suffolk IP12 3DF, UK
and of Boydell & Brewer Inc,
PO Box 41026, Rochester, NY 14604-4126, USA
website: http://www.boydell.co.uk

ISBN 0 85444 044 5

A catalogue record for this book is available
from the British Library

Details of other Surtees Society volumes are available
from Boydell & Brewer Limited

This publication is printed on acid-free paper

Printed in Great Britain by
J. W. Arrowsmith Ltd, Bristol

CONTENTS

ACKNOWLEDGEMENTS

In preparing this manuscript and researching the background of Edmund Tew, we have incurred many obligations. First, we must acknowledge the permission of Jennifer Gill, County Archivist, to publish this notebook from the Durham County Record Office. Moreover, we would also like to thank the following for their assistance and helpful suggestions: David Butler and all the other staff of Durham County Record Office, for their patient service; at Durham University Library, Roger Norris, Linda Drury, and Sheila Doyle; Chris Brooks and Dorothy Hamilton of Durham University; Norma Landau, of the University of California, at Davis; Guy Holborn, Librarian, the Honourable Society of Lincoln's Inn; the staff of the Public Record Office, Kew; the Reverend T.A. Middleton, Rector of Boldon; Nicholas Plumley, Curator, Christ's Hospital.

ABBREVIATIONS

DRO	Durham County Record Office
NRO	Northumberland Record Office
PRO	Public Record Office
TWAS	Tyne and Wear Archives Service

GLOSSARY

General

Affidavit	statement taken under oath
Anker	measure of barrel size, Dutch: 10 old gallons, 8.5 imperial gallons
Ballastheaver/ master	The ballast hills were a large enterprise on the Tyne and the Wear, as a collier (q.v.) could take coal to London, but brought sand back as ballast; charging for depositing the ballast provided a sizeable and profitable business
Beatment	measure made of staved wood, holding a quarter of a peck of two gallons (i.e. about half a gallon)
Besom	broom, or brush made of twigs
Boll	measure of grain in northern England and the Borders, varying from place to place and according to the type of grain being measured; a boll of wheat was usually two bushels, of other grains between four and six
Candlemas	2nd February (Feast of the Purification of the Virgin Mary)
Capuchin	woman's cloak with a hood
Chaldron	a Newcastle chauldron was 53cwt (hundred-weight)
Coble(-man)	local type of small offshore fishing boat
Collier	coastal ship exporting coal, mostly to London
Comber	one who combs woven cloth, usually wool
Committal	see Mittimus

Compounded	settled by a private agreement between the accused and the complainant, usually with payment.
Cranks	of a fire: usually the winding gear for turning spits, but in the North East also a frame for toasting bread
Deal	plank of wood, usually pine or fir
Deposition	statement made under questioning by a magistrate
Earnest	money paid over to bind a bargain
Fitter	agent who sold and loaded the coal from a colliery, who also owned *keels*, and had contracts for loading ships
Fother	generally indicates a horse-drawn cartload, sometimes with regard to coal, one third of a *chaldron*
Garth	enclosed area, field or yard
Geneva	a kind of gin, made in the Netherlands, also called Hollands
Hack	pick axe, usually single-headed, or a fork for raking manure with three or four large teeth at right angles to the long handle
Happing	cloth covering or coverlet
Higler	variation on heckler, one who makes frames for linen weaving
Huckster	street-seller
Indenture	document of agreement between master and apprentice, giving terms and conditions of service and mutual obligations
Invalid	soldier not fully fit for foreign service, often stationed in local barracks or billets
Keel(-man)	local river boat used for loading coal ships (*colliers*), and those who worked on them
Ladyday	25th March (Feast of the Annunciation): until 1752, the official start of the year in old style dating
Lammas	1st August, once observed as a harvest festival

Liberate	order of release (usually from gaol or house of correction)
Manteau	variation on mantua, a loose gown worn by women
Mashfat	mashing vat for grain (in brewing)
Mittimus	order for incarceration (usually in gaol or house of correction)
Moidore	Portuguese gold coin, worth 27 shillings
Note of hand	self-made banknote whose recipient and value were filled in by the payer.
Overman	manager or supervisor in the coalmines, having the daily management of mine, working under a Viewer (q.v.)
Pease	peas, usually boiled to make a dish
Peruka	peruke or wig
Pinfold	public pound for straying cattle
Protection	written protection from the press gang, issued by magistrates to certain local trades such as the keelmen.
Recognizance	undertaking before a justice, whereby a person undertakes both to keep the peace and to fulfil a condition (such as appearing in court, or being bound over to be of good behaviour), and must proffer financial guarantee (surety) in case of default. Usually other parties were required to stand surety by way of support. All money would be forfeited (the recognizance 'estreated') if the conditions were not fulfilled
Salt-officer	one who collected the salt tax and ensured that all salt for sale was taxed
Shift	woman's dress or chemise
Skeel	pail, for milk or water, larger at the base than at the rim, which could be carried on the head; it might hold up to six gallons
Slopseller	seller of clothes (slop was seamen's clothes), mostly ready-made outer garments

Surety	financial guarantee – see Recognizance
Trimmer	in the North East, usually a man who levelled the coal after it had been loaded or poured into a Collier (q.v.)
Truck	either an exchange of goods, or payment in goods, sometimes acquired only at the employer's store
Viewer	chief mine manager or engineer
Vitriol	sulphuric acid or sulphate compound
Wherry(-man)	type of small ship with a shallow draft, usually larger than a *keel*
Whin	gorse or furze
Wort	infusion of malt, for brewing

INTRODUCTION

The attribution of this notebook, now in Durham County Record Office,[1] to the Reverend Edmund Tew, Rector of Boldon, is of long-standing conviction, one clearly shared by the several nineteenth-century owners who wrote inside the front cover. While there is little internal evidence to provide unquestioned proof of Tew's workmanship, there is much, both in the cases referred to, and in the supporting sources for the quarter sessions and assizes, to suggest that Boldon was the origin, and Tew the magistrate. The author talks of 'my parish' in one case, and the sample warrant on the inside of the back cover gives Boldon as the provenance. The cases referred to the assizes for trial were certainly the work of Edmund Tew, whose name is on the extant examinations and depositions of suspects and witnesses. Similar proof of his activities is found in the quarter sessions cases sent to trial.

EDMUND TEW: THE MAN AND HIS CAREER

Edmund Tew, one of four brothers, was born and baptized in Loddington, Northamptonshire, where his father was rector, on 10 January 1700. He was educated at Christ's Hospital, London, where he was a senior student (known as a 'Grecian') in 1715, and followed two of his brothers to Cambridge. He obtained his BA in 1719–20 and MA in 1723, and was a fellow of Jesus College from 1722 to 1730. He was ordained in 1724 by the Bishop of Ely. Subsequently in 1736 he achieved a doctorate in divinity.[2] Tew

1 DRO, D/X 730/1.

2 J. Venn and J.A. Venn (eds), *Alumni Cantabrigienses* (Nendeln, Liechtenstein, 1976), xxx vols, Pt.1, vol. 4, p. 216; J. Foster (ed.), *Alumni Oxonienses: the Members of the University of Oxford, 1715–1886*, xxx vols (Nendeln, Liechtenstein, 1968), vol. 3, p. 1401; E.H. Pearce, *Annals of Christ's Hospital* (London, 1901), p. 85; Durham Diocesan Records, XIV/5, Subscription Book, p. 94 (7 March 1734/5, which also gives the dates when he became deacon and priest).

began his ministry in St. Clement's Cambridge, and was vicar of the parish of Fordham in Cambridgeshire for ten years from 1725, 'where I was too often non-resident and therefore an unworthy vicar', he regretfully recorded in his will.[3] In 1735 he was appointed to the living of the parish of Boldon, and served there for the rest of his life. Boldon, which was in the bishop's gift, was a comparatively wealthy living in the eighteenth century; the parsonage was later famous for its size and architectural sophistication. Tew seems to have been particularly concerned in conflicts over his tithes, which brought in a substantial income.[4] He spent some money on improvements to the parish church, as a blocked door in the south side of the chancel bearing his initials testifies.[5] He died in 1770, and was buried in the vault in Boldon. He was married twice, firstly to Barbara, daughter of Dr Thomas Gibbon, Dean of Carlisle, who died on 26 August 1739, and secondly to Elizabeth who died on 14 August 1764. One daughter died in Boldon in 1740, aged one year four months, shortly after her mother of the same name, and there were two sons, Edward and Edmund. Tew's tombstone records that he was 70 when he died, having been rector of Boldon for 36 years (though in fact it was almost exactly 35 years and six months).[6] Many of the items in his will reflected the sense of obligation acquired during different episodes of his life. He left £4,000 to his old school, Christ's Hospital, on condition that they educated three orphans or sons of poor clergy presented to them by his own family; in addition

3 DRO, D/CG 8/88.

4 W. Fordyce, *The History and Antiquities of the County Palatine of Durham* (Newcastle and London, 1857), 2 vols, vol. 2, p. 736 says the living was worth £653 per annum net. DRO, D/CG 8/86 and 87 records an unsuccessful tithe case over the Gilly Tithes, which had once belonged to Kepier Hospital: R. Surtees, *The History and Antiquities of the County Palatine of Durham etc.* (London, 1820), 2 vols, vol. 2, p. 63.

5 The head of the door is inscribed on three lines, 'E.T. D.D. 1767'.

6 The tombstone evidence in Surtees, *History and Antiquities*, vol. 2, p. 61 is incorrect both about the year of Barbara's death and her father's surname (the extant plaque is a later replacement), but see E. Mackenzie and M. Ross, *An Historical, Topographical and Descriptive View of the County Palatine of Durham etc.* (Newcastle, 1834), 2 vols, vol. 1, p. 71 for a more accurate version of the date. For Thomas Gibbon, see J. Nicholson and R. Burn, *The History and Antiquities of Westmorland and Cumberland* (London, 1778), 2 vols, vol. 2, p. 305, and for his parochial appointment, W. Hutchinson, *The History of the County of Cumberland etc.* (Carlisle, 1794), 2 vols, vol. 1, p. 408.

he left his portrait, which survives and is reproduced here as the frontispiece. Other bequests, to provide books for the poor of Sawbridgeworth (Hertfordshire), and relief for the poor of Fordham (in Cambridgeshire) and Boldon (£20), stemmed from his pastoral career. The list of personal bequests suggests that he was acknowledging the relationships he had established in County Durham not only with gentry and fellow clerics, but also with loyal servants and others such as William Rowland, keelman of Monkwearmouth, who 'muddled away a great deal of money upon my farm at Boldon'. As was conventional, his will made an effort both to provide some acknowledgement, reconciliation or compensation and to make careful provision for his family. In it he mentions his son Edmund, 'who is at this time in bad state of health', and made arrangements in case he, as happened, should predecease him.[7]

Tew was locally active outside his parochial and judicial duties. He served as a governor of Newcastle Infirmary from its inception as a committee formed in early 1751 to establish an institution 'for the sick and lame poor of the counties of Durham, Newcastle upon Tyne and Northumberland'. It opened later that year, admitting its first patients on 8th October.[8] In subsequent years, Tew was one of a large number of governors drawn from a wide range of wealthy and locally influential men such as fellow clergy and magistrates, though they included some from interested groups of relative outsiders such as Durham's Quaker community. Throughout the 1750s he frequently represented County Durham on the House Committee, though his membership did not necessitate attendance at the weekly meetings which admitted and discharged patients, only a handful of members gathering to make these routine decisions. The impression from the attendance records is that those members of the committee who were closer to Newcastle, such as Reverend William Lambe, Rector of Gateshead, were more actively involved on a weekly basis. Still, on three occasions Tew was invited to give the anniversary sermon, preached in the summer to commemorate the

---

7 DRO, D/CG 8/88. The amount to Christ's was to be raised from £2,000 to £4,000 if his son Edmund died before him.

8 *Newcastle Courant* 2988, 30 March 1751; TWAS, HO/RVI/114, item twelve, 'An Account of the Infirmary for the Sick and Lame Poor etc.' We are indebted to Dorothy Hamilton for these Infirmary references.

foundation of the infirmary, and the text of his 1756 discourse – on the necessary relationship between frugality and charity – survives. In 1769 he gave the hospital £100, the interest of which was to be used for a ward for incurables.[9] Tew was also consistently involved in other charitable causes, such as the Sons of the Clergy who raised money for clergymen's widows and orphans. He preached a heartfelt sermon at their annual meeting in 1737, and in the 1760s was reported to have donated two gifts of £100 to their funds. His preaching activities extended to the Cumberland assizes in Carlisle where in 1750 he discussed 'the Queen of Sheba's Notions of Government'.[10]

Tew and the Community

While Boldon was his centre, the business of this justice ranged across the increasingly populous and turbulent communities at the mouths of the North-East's two most important rivers, the Tyne and the Wear. In the mid-eighteenth century Boldon was a small rural village strung along the main Sunderland–Newcastle road, sufficiently scattered to have been divided into the townships of East and West Boldon. Although lacking any major sources of wealth, it attracted some more prosperous families whose fine houses still survive in the main street. In 1736, according to Bishop Chandler's survey, the parish contained about 80 families and fewer than 400 people, while Whitburn, its neighbour nearer the coast to the east, had more than 100 families. Most people in Boldon were Anglicans, there being only two Presbyterian families, and none were recorded as Catholic.[11] Alto-

9 E. Mackenzie, *A Descriptive and Historical Account of the Town and Country of Newcastle upon Tyne, including the Borough of Gateshead* (Newcastle upon Tyne, 1827), p. 510.

10 TWAS HO/RVI/2/1-4, unpaginated; see HO/RVI/2/3, 14 February 1760. Tew also attended one of the special court of governors in 1760. The sermon is in HO/RVI/114 item 1, 'Frugality the Support of Charity'. He was invited to give sermons in both 1753 and 1754 too, though none survive – the latter was in fact given by Thomas Dockwray, extant as item 9 in HO/RVI/114. See HO/RVI/2/1, 26 April 1753, HO/RVI/2/2, 2 April 1754, *Newcastle Courant* 4485, 4 September 1762, and the sermons in Newcastle Central Library, *A Sermon Preach'd Before the Sons of the Clergy* (London, 1737), and *The Queen of Sheba's Notions of Government Considered etc.* (Newcastle upon Tyne, n.d. probably 1750).

11 *Bishop Chandler's Notes of a Visitation in 1736*, Newcastle Central Library; P. Brassley, *The Agricultural Economy of Northumberland and Durham* (New York

gether, there must have been more than 1,000 people in these communities, and it is perhaps surprising that less than a tenth of Tew's business derived from them. He was accustomed to dealing with people from many parts of the country, as the trade of the north-east coast attracted many from seaport towns in England and Scotland. For example, some of the employment problems of unpaid wages and abused apprentices arose from ships docked on the Tyne or the Wear, skippered by men from Whitby, Scarborough and Great Yarmouth. Tew must have been known and been available to those who brought cases to magistrates, particularly the local constables, as well as to the wider community. His notebook records business brought to him, or ordered by him, involving constables from a large area, including Boldon, Whitburn, Chester-le-Street, Monkwearmouth (mostly from the 'Shoreside', the northern side of the Wear), Sunderland, and South Shields (including various parts of it such as East Pan Ward and Westoe).[12] Overwhelmingly, though, the bulk of Tew's work stemmed from the complaints of inhabitants living along the two great rivers of the North-East, the Tyne and Wear, several miles to the north and south of Boldon. Indeed, whether because of Boldon's position mid-way between the two rivers, or Tew's personal accessibility, or a general shortage of magistrates, or their absence from home, a great many complaints, nearly four-fifths of the whole recorded in the notebook, came from these larger parishes.[13] Despite his rural location, therefore, the bulk of Tew's business originated from these areas of rapid urbanization. The three parishes of Sunderland, Monkwearmouth and South Shields alone produced more than two-thirds of those bringing cases to him.

These riverside communities were very different from the rural parish of Boldon, where farming predominated. Both rivers showed a similar pattern of growth at the estuary mouth, reflecting a diversion of maritime business away from Newc-

---

and London, 1985), pp. 191–3, uses a high multiplier of 4.75, while Chandler's own population totals, which very exceptionally he provides for Rothbury, suggest a somewhat lower figure of about 4.4 persons per household.

12 See Surtees, *History and Antiquities*, vol. 2, p. 94 for the three constabularies.

13 To judge from his notebook, Tew was unavailable during the spring or late autumn months of 1751, 1752, 1753, 1756, 1757 and 1758. He spent some time in Bath.

astle itself.[14] The developing economy here presented problems of unpredictable industries, seasonal employment, rapid growth, and industrial protest. Everywhere there was a fluctuating population of seafarers, their taverns and lodging houses a perpetual source of trouble. The Tyneside parishes of Hebburn, Jarrow and South Shields, together with some smaller places to the north between Boldon and the river, provided an increasing part of his activities over the years, and by the 1760s exceeded the contribution of the Wearside communities. The most important industry in the area was salt, produced by boiling seawater in pans. In 1760 there were 140 pans in South Shields, concentrated around the area of Mill Dam and Stone Quay. The largest single owner was Lord Ravensworth (with 26), but smaller numbers were owned by people mentioned in Tew's notebook such as Nicholas Fairless, John Cookson and the firm of Cookson and Deere. Total production from these pans was more than 70,000 tons, compared with fewer than 2,500 in Sunderland.[15] The industry in its decline was far from tranquil. In 1743 a number of wealthy residents from South Shields, 'a sea port in the County of Durham', fearful of disorder, petitioned the Secretary of State, the Duke of Newcastle, on behalf of the inhabitants, requesting the permanent stationing of troops in the town. The salt trade, they said, had much declined in recent years, the ships were idle in the winter months, and many were out of work.

> The said people being of a riotous and mutinous disposition, especially those employed in the salt work, having about four years ago assembled themselves together in a riotous manner to the number of several hundreds, to the loss and damage of many of the Inhabitants, and doth now threaten to do the same.[16]

Little of this emerges in Tew's notebook, but the many saltworkers, and their employers, and the individual problems they pro-

---

14 B. Dietz, 'The North-East Coal Trade, 1550–1750: Measures, Markets and the Metropolis', *Northern History*, 22, 1986, pp. 280–94; J.M. Ellis, 'Cartels in the Coal Industry on Tyneside, 1699–1750', *Northern History*, 34, 1998, pp. 134–48.

15 G.B. Hodgson, *The Borough of South Shields from the Earliest Times to the Close of the Nineteenth Century* (Newcastle upon Tyne, 1903), p. 116.

16 PRO, SP 36/62/188 9. On the 1740 regional riots which provoked this anxiety, see G. Morgan and P. Rushton, *Rogues, Thieves and the Rule of Law: the Problem of Law Enforcement in North-East England, 1718–1800* (London, 1998), pp. 197–8.

duced for each other, reflect the dominance of this industry. One of the signatories to this petition was John Burdon, described by one local historian as 'then the principal magistrate in South Shields'. But, as Tew records in his notebook, in 1757 Burdon went to live at Hardwick Hall near Sedgefield, leaving South Shields short of magistrates.[17] This shortage resurfaced in the tempestuous 1790s, when his son Rowland Burdon, MP for the area, was central in raising local complaint about the absence of resident magistrates.[18] With glass production, shipping and other seafaring services which supported a large population of seamen, South Shields was growing throughout the century: omitted from Bishop Chandler's survey, it rivalled Sunderland in population by 1801.[19]

The parishes of the Wear were different again. The northern side, Monkwearmouth, was probably fairly small in the middle of the eighteenth century, while the two parishes on the south, Sunderland and Bishopwearmouth, together contained at least 8,000 people, producing a 'small-scale version of Newcastle'.[20] Increasingly, shifting coal into the ships and out of the port came to dominate the local economy. There was still some salt panning (Pans Bank on the south side offers a reminder), and other seafaring trades such as glassmaking, potteries, ropemaking and shipbuilding were growing, but the local keelmen were the dominant group both in the population and in the many disturbances which punctuated the century. In the eighteenth century the growth was mostly on the southern side of the river, where the waggonways and other forms of transport brought coal to the ships from the mines being opened up further inland. Unlike South Shields and

17 Hodgson, *Borough of South Shields*, p. 122; J. Ellis, 'The Decline and Fall of the Tyneside Salt Industry, 1660–1790: A Re-Examination', *Economic History Review*, 33 (1), 1980, pp. 45–58; Notebook (using Tew's own style of dates): February 19th 1757.

18 PRO, HO 42/22/261, 42/164-5 and 549.

19 A.E. Smailes, *North England* (London, 1968), p. 146; D.J. Rowe, 'The North-East', in F.M.L. Thompson (ed.), *The Cambridge Social History of Britain, 1750–1790*, 3 vols, vol. 1, *Regions and Communities* (Cambridge, 1990), pp. 419–22.

20 Rowe, 'The North-East', p. 419; 550 families in Sunderland in 1719 could not pay rates. If they amounted to the usual 45% who were poor, there were probably 1,200 families in all or about 5,800 people: DRO, EP/Su.Ht., 7/1. There were 440 families in Bishopwearmouth according to Chandler, 1736; see Brassley, *Agricultural Economy*, pp. 191–3 and *Bishop Chandler's Notes*.

probably Monkwearmouth, Sunderland and Bishopwearmouth were served by several busy magistrates with whom Tew cooperated.[21]

The Church and the Magistracy

Clerical justices were not unusual in mid-eighteenth-century England, and were in fact steadily increasing in the period of Tew's service. While this was a national trend, it seems to have taken an exaggerated form in County Durham, where the influence of the Bishop over appointments remained strong. By the early nineteenth century clergymen made up an unprecedented proportion of the commission of the peace for the county.[22] The status of these clerical magistrates was not always one of full integration with the central group of the commission, the quorum. This had originally been a select group of justices supposedly more learned in the law, and exclusion from it had occasioned fierce disputes in the seventeenth century. While there was a trend by the early eighteenth century to include all magistrates in the quorum, it seems that at the start of the reign of George III, when all commissions of the peace were renewed, 'almost every commission ended with a special section devoted to judicial brethren of the cloth, two of whom would be the only justices in the commission not of the quorum'. Generally this was true of Tew's service, for he never matched the full involvement on the commission which was achieved by long-serving clerics such as William Lambe, John Ellison (of Bedlington, Durham's outpost in Northumberland) and John Emmerson (of Winston). In this sense,

---

21 Teasdale Mowbray, referred to in the notebook on July 29th 1760 and December 29th 1762, lived in a fine house at Bishopwearmouth Green. Other justices were Robert Hutton, George Baker and Matthew Carr; the first two lived further away. See Rain's plan: M. Clay, G. Milburn and S. Miller (eds), *An Eye Plan of Sunderland and Bishopwearmouth 1785–1790, by John Rain* (Newcastle upon Tyne, 1984), p. 43.

22 N. Landau, *The Justices of the Peace, 1679–1760* (Berkeley, 1984), p. 143; W.B. Maynard, 'The Ecclesiastical Administration of the Archdeaconry of Durham, 1774–1856' (unpublished Ph.D., University of Durham, 1973), pp. 27–8, 92; C.M. Fraser and K. Emsley, 'The Clerical Justices of the Peace in the North East, 1626–30', *Archaeologia Aeliana*, 5th series, 2, 1974, pp. 189–99. PRO, C192/2 indicates that while there were eight clergy on the commission in the 1750s and twelve in the 1770s, the number was nearer forty by the 1820s (38 in 1820).

it can be said, he was never a member of the inner group of Durham justices.[23]

Nevertheless, Tew, a magistrate from 1750, served on the commission of the peace officially until his death, and in practical terms at least until the late 1760s. The notebook therefore covers the bulk of his active years as a justice, 1750–64, and reflects a very busy life of judicial and other duties. He was listed in the 1750 commission of the peace, drawn up in early summer, but the fee for his *dedimus potestatem*, the official grant of authority by the Lord Chancellor, was not paid until October: he began recording his 'account of business' in this notebook from the following month.[24] Tew made appearances at the quarter sessions throughout the period of the notebook, though not at every one. He was recorded as attending at least one sessions in every year from 1752 to 1764, and in 1762 was at all four. Generally he attended two each year, but in 1757 and 1758, was at only one. There may have been deliberate reasons for his attendance, connected to the cases coming to the court: it is certain that he was there when any serious case produced under his authority came before a quarter sessions jury. For example, he is recorded as present when a man was sentenced to whipping for theft in October 1763, and when two women thieves were sentenced to transportation in January 1764. This seems to have been his custom throughout the period of the notebook. Whether he sat in judgement in 'his' cases is unclear; there were few guidelines concerning the ethical problems of doing so in the published handbooks of advice to justices. In addition to attending the sessions or its adjournments, he also participated in two of the ad hoc committees set up by the magistrates to review problems. He was listed as one of those inspecting the state of Durham's house of correction in 1752, and in that year and 1754, helped inspect

23 Landau, *Justices of the Peace*, p. 143; see also pp. 136 and 339. PRO, C192/2, part 1, records the increasing involvement of clerics in the more selective commissions of pleas and gaol delivery in the 1750s and 1760s, though earlier records (in part 2) indicate that one or two clergymen had been more centrally involved in earlier times such as the 1730s. See G. Jacob, *A New Law-Dictionary etc.*, 10th edition, enlarged by J. Morgan (London, 1782), under 'quorum'.

24 PRO, C193/45, 15 October 1750; C192/2, part 2, the commission lists were dated 21 May 1750, and endorsed on 3 July: Tew's name has apparently been inserted afterwards.

the state of local bridges in Durham and Chester-le-Street. This appears to have been a low rate of participation in these committees, compared with the involvement of some other justices. His public judicial activities seem to have declined substantially after 1764, though he was once recorded at the sessions in 1766, and still sent cases to trial. His last known indictments were in 1767 and 1769, by which time he was not recorded as attending the sessions.[25] His presence at the sessions may not always have been possible, for it is clear from gaps in the notebook that in a number of years he was either inactive or unavailable for some months at a time. His comment in his will when leaving a legacy to an 'honest servant' in Bath who gave 'careful attendance' on him (and his wife) may indicate his whereabouts in these periods.[26]

Justices of the Peace and the Process of Law Enforcement

The primary role of twentieth-century justices of the peace is to hear and decide on charges brought before them: overwhelmingly their activities are public and judicial. In the early modern period, by contrast, magistrates spent far more time hearing allegations in their own homes or in relatively informal settings such as inns, and taking actions which more closely approximate to that of a modern police force – interviewing complainants and witnesses, signing warrants for arrest, summoning the accused to appear before them to answer complaints, and deciding on the nature of any charges to be brought. Much of this was essentially done in private. They also had the powers of summary conviction and punishment in certain areas. Much of this activity was confined to the immediate community, rarely being referred upwards to the quarter sessions, and, with the exception of notebooks like this, virtually unrecorded.[27] The law encouraged magistrates to conduct a great deal of business 'out of sessions', and these proceedings became both more formal and more cent-

---

25 DRO, Q/S/OM 5, 15 July 1752, and Q/S/OB, 11, pp. 43, 108, 116, 118, 130, 194, 212, 224, 284; Q/S/OB 12, pp. 1, 14, 32, 43, 62, 74, 99, 114, 124, 135, 145, 179, 193, 214, 228, 243; QS/O/B 13, pp. 89 and 119; PRO, DURH 17/10 (George Bewick, 1769). The only case Tew missed was that of reluctant overseer Joseph Topcliffe.

26 DRO, D/CG 8/88.

27 For a systematic study of some of the surviving notebooks, see D. Oberwittler, 'Crime and Authority in Eighteenth-Century England: Law Enforcement on the Local Level', *Historical Social Research*, 15 (2), 1990, pp. 3–34.

ral to law enforcement during the course of the eighteenth century. Some proceedings such as the licensing sessions for regulating alehouses were specialised affairs, held at least once a year in each district. In Northumberland, these were regarded as adjournments of the full quarter sessions, travelling to most areas of the county. Similar adjournments with two or more justices present were held in Durham City in between the full sessions to deal with a range of routine duties such as the appointment of gamekeepers, release of debtors, and minor offences. There were several of these a year, varying according to need. Other local processes, such as the petty sessions, also involving at least a pair of justices sitting together, were regularly advertised, and acquired a greater role in handling minor offences. The long gaps between the quarter sessions left a continual need for swifter justice for more minor problems, and increasingly petty sessions fulfilled this purpose. Their 'establishment, growth and consolidation', it has been said, was the most important development in the structure of eighteenth-century local government.[28] Unfortunately, few records survive of these proceedings in County Durham except notification of their meetings. In the 1750s petty sessions were held only once a year in Durham, Houghton-le-Spring, Chester-le-Street, Bishop Auckland, and Stockton, usually in April or May. These times were agreed at the quarterly meetings and recorded in the rough order books. Towards the end of the eighteenth century, they were advertized in the newspapers as being held fortnightly in Durham city (in the Court Coffee House). The substance of their proceedings must remain speculative, though there are indications that those convicted before two justices in this way sometimes appealed to the full quarter sessions to overturn their convictions, usually unsuccessfully.[29]

Finally, there was the lone justice out of sessions: he was the first person complainants turned to, and was the primary source of warrants, formal inquiries, and indictments. Also, much business involving Poor Law settlements, payment of relief, alehouse irregularities such as unlicensed tippling, were, if not under the complete control of a single justice, at least allocated to him in

---

28 Landau, *Justices of the Peace*, p.206, and ch. 7, p. 209ff.

29 DRO, Q/S/OM 4 and 5 (unpaginated); Q/S/OB 10, pp. 292-3; *Newcastle Courant* 5531, 12 October 1782. Four men appealed separately against conviction before Henry Lambton and George Baker.

the early stages of a complaint. He could recommend a solution, even if he needed the support of another justice or the quarter sessions proper. According to the traditional 'Arcadian concept of judicial paternalism', he was the father figure of the English legal system, the source of wisdom and mediation, judgement and guidance.[30] The surviving notebooks illustrate that in some respects this idealized image was perhaps half-true, as justices clearly acted to re-establish peace in their neighbourhoods, negotiating and mediating settlements to disputes, and censoring anti-social behaviour without formal prosecution. Yet this highly personal regime was not without its dangers. Tew, like other justices, was subject to insults from those he tried to control, two of whom he incarcerated for short periods until they were willing to make public apology. John Bridon said he had not had justice in a dispute with a local constable, and was locked up in Durham gaol until Tew released him 'upon falling on his knees and paying 10s'. John Bell called Tew a fool and threatened him with a suit in the King's Bench, but after the intercession of his friends, was released from gaol after he had apologised in front of 'all my parish and the constable'. The support of the courts was sometimes required to reinforce the lesson: Richard Matthew, accused of drunkenness and assault, was summarily fined 5s by Tew, but when he entered a recognizance 'did insult and grossly abuse' him, and therefore, by a later decision of the quarter sessions, forfeited his surety money.[31] Physical assault is not recorded here, but in 1742 the Northumberland justice Edward Blackett reported to his fellow members of the bench that he had had to gaol Thomas Fenwick because, when brought before him, he had threatened violence to 'several persons of my family and it was by force he was restrained from proceeding to blows even in my presence'. That this kind of aggression was not unusual is suggested by the behaviour of Durham man John Mills, under arrest in 1731. He claimed he had '23 or more persons, his confederates'

---

30 Landau, *Justices of the Peace*, p. 173; for the contexts in which people went to law, see M.J. Ingram, 'Communities and Courts: Law and Disorder in Early-Seventeenth-Century Wiltshire', in J.S. Cockburn (ed.), *Crime in England, 1550–1800* (London, 1977), pp. 111–34.

31 See the Notebook references to John Bridon, October 15th 1755; John Bell, November 23rd 1756; Richard Matthew, September 26th 1754, and DRO, Q/S/OB 11, p. 111.

who were strong enough to attack the justices who had committed him, and threatened a witness that he would bring as many as were needed to burn the town where he lived.[32]

The Notebook as Evidence of a JP's Activities

While conforming to no uniform pattern, notebooks such as Tew's, which justices were encouraged to maintain, show the business which came to their own home. They reveal the magistrate's role, not just in prosecuting crimes and pursuing criminals through the courts, but in administering the poor law, regulating conditions of employment, and mediating and settling personal disputes. Ensuring that individuals performed their duties to the parishes in this and other areas formed one local task for the individual justice. Most actions, however, involved resolving individual problems, and ensuring good community order rather than prosecuting offenders. As such, justices' notebooks help to resolve the apparent paradox of early modern England, whose population seems to have been so litigious, that while many turned to the law, few went to court. Tew's notebook consists largely of brief summaries of the warrants he took out on hearing complaints, the nature of the wrong complained of, and, in most cases, the outcome in terms of either reconciliation between the parties or dismissal of the validity of the accusation. The resulting list provides a picture of the huge number of offended victims who turned to a magistrate for justice, demanding that those who had given offence be forced to answer for their behaviour. The notebook recorded warrants and solutions rather than lengthy testimony taken for court appearances, though these were certainly produced for trial cases; no references are made to the petty sessions. In style and structure, Tew's notebook most closely resembles that of his near contemporary, William Hunt of Wiltshire.[33]

---

32 NRO, QSB 85, Epiphany 1741/2, f. 73; PRO, DURH 17/4, 7 May 1731.

33 E. Crittall (ed.), *The Justicing Notebook of William Hunt, 1744–49*, Wiltshire Record Society (Devizes, 1982); E. Silverthorne (ed.), *The Deposition Book of Richard Wyatt, J.P., 1767–1776*, Surrey Record Society, vol. 30 (Guildford, 1978); R. Paley (ed.), *Justice in Eighteenth-Century Hackney: the Justicing Notebook of Henry Norris and the Hackney Petty Sessions Book*, London Record Society, vol. 28 (London, 1981). The pattern was already old, see C. Read (ed.), *William Lambarde and Local Government: His 'Ephemeris' and Twenty-Nine Charges to Juries and Commissions* (Ithaca, NY, 1962).

The procedure Tew followed closely matched that recommended in the justices' handbooks which were widely available and popular at the time.[34] His customary action was issuing a warrant, which was used to force someone to come and face a complaint. Tew wrote out more than a thousand, broadly divided into general and special warrants. The majority were special warrants, designed to give defendants a clear idea of the likely charge which could be brought; equally important was the rule that those named in the special warrants had to come before the magistrate who issued them, thus ensuring that he retained control over the outcome. General warrants could avoid being specific about the likely charge, and perhaps favoured a process which left things rather vague, allowing the justice to make up his mind on the presentations before him whether there was in fact anything at all which required his further action. Usually there are few references here to the stage which would customarily have succeeded the warrant and the appearance before the magistrate: recognizances or sureties. Most of the recognizances recorded in the notebook were designed to deal with the few cases which Tew sent to, or intended for, the courts.[35]

In addition to issuing warrants, Tew wrote dozens of letters about various matters, usually to Poor Law officials or employers, either making inquiries or issuing instructions. The substance of these is given in the notebook. In enforcing the legislation controlling alehouses, he withdrew or issued licences, and fined illegal sellers of ale the usual 20s, which the law he cites from Charles I's reign allowed him to give to the poor.[36] He sometimes carefully divided the money between the poor of several places. He also ordered the removal of more than 30 paupers back to their

---

34 R. Burn, *The Justice of the Peace and Parish Officer*, 6th edition, 3 vols (London, 1758), vol. 3, pp. 430–1.

35 Most of Tew's recognizances are for court appearances, most of the sureties for release from custody in gaol or House of Correction. Note that his library contained many legal handbooks as well as theological works, including Burn's *The Justice of the Peace*, and Jacob's law dictionary: *A Catalogue of the Library of the Late Rev. Dr Tew, Rector of Bolden* (Newcastle upon Tyne, 1770), to be found in Durham University Library, Collection of Old Catalogues, which also has a supplementary catalogue by bookseller W. Charnley of the items omitted from this list.

36 3 Charles I, c.3; Burn, *The Justice of the Peace*, vol. 1, pp. 22–3.

parishes of settlement, though some of these orders may have been beyond the full letter of his authority. In theory, while a complaint about settlement could be made to one justice, an order for removal should strictly have been given by two. On a few occasions he mentions other magistrates, and in one instance worked in harness with John Fenwick to take a recognizance in a felony accusation. This was the pattern in other localities such as Sunderland and Monkwearmouth, where pairs of justices often worked on legal problems. Tew realized that he had not followed the proper legal procedure in one case, when he authorized the seizure of a tenant's goods in lieu of rent: 'this warrant should have been signed by two Justices', he admits. There remains great uncertainty, however, whether any penalties could be imposed on justices for behaving in what was technically an illegal as well as a high-handed manner. Historians have not been able to find records of any severe consequences.[37]

The bulk of Tew's business consisted of complaints by victims about the behaviour of neighbours, employers or family members. Many seem to have been serious: assault, often extremely violent, was a common item. Some allegations involved rape. Both servants and apprentices reported complaints of abuse of a broader kind against their masters or mistresses, also in many instances involving violence. In addition, many thefts or losses of goods were alleged, as was their acquisition by unsuspecting dealers and buyers. Much of this could have come before any quarter sessions: indeed, the substance of accusations recorded by Tew seems to have been almost indistinguishable from that of cases tried at the county level on formal indictments. For example, nothing seems to have come of one incident in which goods were stolen from a wrecked ship: yet in the quarter sessions of both Northumberland and Durham in the eighteenth century, identical cases of this kind were punished severely.[38]

---

37 See Notebook, quotation from December 9th 1756; Burn, *The Justice of the Peace*, vol. 3, pp. 80–1, 85 and 94; N. Landau, 'Who was Subjected to the Laws of Settlement? Procedure under the Settlement Law in Eighteenth-Century England', *Agricultural History Review*, 43 (2), 1995, pp. 139–59, p. 147 and particularly note 39.

38 Notebook, October 19th 1763, wreck of the *Industry*, and search of houses in South Shields; NRO, QSO, 9, pp. 92, 115–16, men from near Amble prosecuted for stealing shipwrecked goods in 1755.

Crimes and Trials

The remarkable feature of Tew's activities is how few of his cases came to court: despite more than 1,000 warrants, very few of the accusations came to trial. Only 21 people in Tew's notebook can be found in the records of the assizes and quarter sessions, although there are more than 60 references suggesting that he was intending to send cases to the courts. In addition, he prepared indictments for two further cases after 1764. In all, only 18 people were tried, five at the assizes, and 13 at the quarter sessions: two charges failed for 'want of prosecution'. They were an accurate reflection of both the serious and the relatively trivial affairs which came to the notice of local magistrates. Less than a tenth of the complaints Tew heard could be construed as accusations of felonies or serious misdemeanours: theft was a particularly rare allegation.

At the assizes, four women were charged with offences related to theft. One, Lucy Mills of Whitburn, was prosecuted on a warrant from Tew for breaking and entering Mary Shepherd's house, and stealing some meal. Servant Mary Grainger was charged with theft of goods from shopkeeper Martha Ayre, her master's daughter, and the probable instigator of the crime, Jane Maugham, was accused of receiving them. Mary Thompson allegedly stole a cap, knot and buckles from Mary Read, wife of a Gateshead labourer. In the most serious case which Tew sent to the assizes, William Neesham (or Neasham) was charged with the rape of 'an infant' aged ten, Sarah Turner, in Sunderland workhouse, to whom he gave the 'foul distemper'. Committed to gaol by Anthony Wilkinson, Neesham was acquitted at his trial, despite poignant evidence provided by the young victim and a surgeon. One of the accused thieves, singlewoman Lucy Mills was equally fortunate in being found not guilty: there may have been doubt about her means of entry into the house, as she had apparently found a hidden key for the door and therefore could not have broken in. The two collaborators, spinster Mary Grainger and Jane, wife of William Maugham (or Mangham) were not so lucky in 1763. Grainger pleaded guilty to grand larceny with benefit of clergy, and was branded in the hand, while Maugham was transported for 14 years for receiving. Mary Thompson was also convicted for stealing and transported.[39]

---

39 Notebook, William Neesham, July 22nd 1754; Lucy Mills, July 22nd 1755; Mary Grainger and Jane Maugham, October 11th 1763; Mary Thompson, July 31st 1764; Assize records PRO, DURH 17/7, 22 July 1754 (Neesham) and 22 June

The quarter sessions cases sent to trial by Tew reflected the greater variety of offences found in this lower court in the period: many indictments in the region involved felonies, certainly, but far more concerned non-felonious charges such as assault, unneighbourly conduct, Poor Law and vagrancy offences, and failures to perform public duty or accept public office. As a result of Tew's actions, five people were convicted for petty larceny: Richard Harrison was whipped in 1754 and sent back to Battersea, Elisabeth Robinson and two women working together, Margaret Wanless and Jane Ottley, were all transported at the January 1764 sessions, and Jane Maxfield was whipped in 1764. Of these Margaret Wanless (or Wandless) is the most interesting, because she appears to have stood trial rather than her young son Martin: Tew regards her as receiving the goods stolen by Martin, but he was not tried on any charge. During the time she spent in Durham gaol awaiting shipment, more than a year, she bore a daughter Dorothy who had to be maintained at county expense until transferred to her father in 1767, the year after her mother's transportation. Wanless was also unusual in appealing from gaol to the Secretary of State against her sentence, one of the few quarter sessions transportees to do so, but was unsuccessful.[40]

Three women were involved in a bawdy house – Ann Coarser or Carson, fined 2s 6d in 1762 for running it, and two women, Ann Rogers and Alice Murray for frequenting the house; the latter were discharged for want of prosecution, perhaps because no specific witnesses were bound over to appear in their case. Coarser faced accusations by a householder and one of the overseers. Failure to pursue this kind of prosecution, however, was not unusual: in a similar case, the notebook records that two women accused of keeping a bawdy house, Mary Hannah and

---

1755 (Mills); DURH 17/9, 11 October 1763 (Grainger and Maugham) and 31 July 1764 (Thompson). Buckles and handkerchiefs (the latter often substantial pieces of silk or fine linen) were highly valued because they were some of the few personal items made of precious materials.

40 Notebook, October 16th 1753, and DRO, Q/S/OB 11, p. 72 (Harrison); Notebook, October 17th, 18th and 21st 1763, and DRO, Q/S/OB 12, p. 218, Q/S/OB 13, p.108 (Robinson, Wanless and Ottley); Notebook, 19 January 1767, and PRO, SP 44/87/303, and 308 for her mother's appeal (Dorothy Wandless); Notebook, July 21st 1764, and DRO, Q/S/OB 12, p. 264 (Jane Maxfield). For women and crime, see Morgan and Rushton, *Rogues, Thieves and the Rule of Law*, ch. 5.

Isable Porteous, escaped trial because 'the overseers agreed with them to drop the prosecution'.[41]

There were three assault convictions resulting in fines: two, John Green, a Sunderland attorney, and Nicholas Swan, a member of a press gang, were in some way public figures. Swan was given the heavy fine of £5, and remained in gaol until he found the money. Green, too, suffered this penalty when he later turned his violence against senior magistrate George Baker. This was in marked contrast to the usual run of small fines for assault in the quarter sessions, involving a few shillings at the most. It is likely that the men's status, rather than the offence, was an issue here: one was a professional and the other had local authority, and so both might expect heavier punishment for misbehaviour if it was thought to constitute betrayal or abuse of their position. Heavy fines were reserved for assaults involving firearms, serious injury, or army and excise officers, local officials and others of higher than average social standing.[42]

Finally, two quarter sessions cases are a little obscure because neither the notebook or the quarter sessions records provide much detail. It is likely that Tew's Joseph Topcliff, a master mariner recorded as being bound over on Robert Hutton's warrant on 8 November 1763, is the Joseph Topcliffe fined at the quarter sessions in October 1764 for refusing to serve as overseer in Monkwearmouth. Joseph Yellowly, fined 6d at the sessions, is also recorded as the result of Hutton's warrant, but the nature of his offence is nowhere specified.[43]

Failures and Negotiated Justice

Of the cases where some intention to prosecute is recorded, but which did not appear in court, Tew recorded some explanations on 13 occasions. Two each were 'withdrawn', 'released', or 'dropped', and seven were 'superseded'. Sometimes he used the threat of prosecution to produce a desirable outcome: William

---

41 Notebook, July 21st 1762 and DRO, Q/S/OB 12, p.150; Notebook, August 31st 1756 (Hannah and Porteous). Ann Coarser was publicly whipped in 1752 for an unspecified felony, DRO, Q/S/OB 10, p. 314, Q/S/OM 5, April sessions.

42 Notebook, April 13th 1752, and DRO, Q/S/OB 10, pp. 323-5 and 332 (Green); Notebook, May 18th and June 14th 1759, and DRO, Q/S/OB 12, p. 15 (Swan).

43 Notebook, November 8th 1763, and DRO, Q/S/OB 12, p.278 (Topcliff); Notebook, June 10th 1762 and DRO, Q/S/OB 12, p. 142 (Yellowly).

Forster, servant to Robert Thompson, was the father of a bastard child born to Ann Humble. Substantial recognizances, including one of £20 for him, were taken out for his appearance at the quarter sessions, but the marginal note explains simply that 'he marryed her'.[44]

Many complaints did not go as far as recognizances or committals to gaol. In a large number of cases no outcome or decision is recorded, but in more than a third of those where he seems to have seen the case to a conclusion, Tew simply marks them 'agreed'. Sometimes these agreements between the parties also involved monetary compensation. Typically, one case of theft was 'made up' between the parties for compensation of 6s 10d. Similarly, an accusation of attempted rape made apparently by the same person, a servant maid against her master George Man, was resolved in exchange for a year's salary and Man 'dismissing her'. In this practice of negotiated settlement, Tew was following the recommendations of contemporary justices' handbooks. Richard Burn, also a northern clerical magistrate (in Westmorland), suggested in his much reprinted handbook that

> in the conduct of trials of trespasses and assaults, the court frequently recommends the defendant to talk with the prosecutor, that is, to make amends for the injury done him; and if the prosecutor comes and acknowledges a satisfaction received, the court will set a small fine on the defendant as 3s 4d or 12d.[45]

If the two sides had come to an agreement before the indictment was brought into court, the defendant was supposed to enter a plea of guilty, supported by a witness to the deal, and be officially released by the magistrates. However, Tew's notebook indicates that few of the cases settled in this way were returned to the courts. Some, in fact, seem to have been settled so privately that only a vague report had been made to him ('as I hear' he records in one agreed case). By mediating and encouraging people to settle out of court, Tew was perhaps ensuring that quarter sessions business was kept to a minimum.[46] In a smaller number of cases, Tew records the result as 'superseded': in theory this should have indicated that the person named in the warrant had

44 Notebook, May 10th 1756.

45 Notebook, August 26th 1751 and July 26th 1754; Burn, *The Justice of the Peace*, vol. 3, p. 278.

46 Notebook, November 25th 1758.

come before him and found sufficient surety for his or her behaviour (resulting in an order *supersedeas*, allowing the person to be free from arrest if the same complainant went to another justice). More generally, the term had a formal meaning of a justice's decision to halt proceedings, either on the good grounds that guarantees had been given that the offensive behaviour would not recur, or because there was no case to answer.[47]

Summary Justice

In general, there were few penalties imposed by Tew without formal prosecution, apart from those on alehouse offenders. One unnamed woman 'rogue' from South Shields was ordered to be whipped by the constable of West Boldon and sent back to her parish with a pass. Otherwise, there were a few examples of Tew sentencing people to periods in the stocks, mostly for drunkenness. The use of the stocks for humiliating community punishments is typical of the rarely-reported penalties for which justices' notebooks provide a vital evidence. Almost the first order recorded by Tew was the repair of the stocks, though he used them only three times, sentencing two men and two women for up to six hours.[48]

In addition, Tew ordered many people to the gaol or house of correction. Partly these were also examples of summary conviction: disobedient servants and apprentices were a particular target, being incarcerated (probably with hard labour) for up to a month. More commonly, however, it was the result of an accused's inability to raise sufficient guarantees (sureties) for their good behaviour, supported by two others with similar financial resources. Frequently, the phrase 'for want of sureties' accompanied such an order. This suggests that the main use of incarceration was as a kind of deterrent against those who could not underwrite their appearance financially, or find friends and family to back them with money. Such people had better remain out of trouble, and avoid attracting complaints before the justices.

---

47 Burn, *The Justice of the Peace*, vol. 3, pp. 334, 361; Thomas Potts, *A Compendious Law Dictionary etc.* (London, 1813), p. 677.

48 Notebook, February 20th 1764 (rogue whipped), November 16th 1750, June 16th 1754, October 13th 1762 and September 7th 1763 (stocks).

Regulation

In addition to the routine duty of signing the book which set the poor rate in the parish, many particular Poor Law problems came before Tew. Some unmarried women swore statements concerning the fathers of their children, and Tew was required to follow up the matter by taking out a warrant against the men. His powers in bastardy cases were considerable. According to a recent law of 1733, any man 'charged on oath with being the father of a bastard child shall be apprehended and committed to gaol until he gives security to indemnify the parish from expense'.[49] While Tew managed to induce most men to produce offers of either money or marriage, the justice's authority was not always effective: one man ran away after agreeing to marry the mother of the child. Tew made many orders for maintenance (a few concerning the mentally disabled described as lunatics and idiots), frequently when this had been refused by parish officials or family members. Finally, he explored the settlement of many people in need. The farthest removals recorded in the notebook were to Birmingham and the Devonshire parish of Dartmouth.[50]

Other matters of community regulation involved the maintenance and repair of local highways, usually necessitating the enforcement of parishioners' duties to work so many days a year in repairing roads. The surveyor of highways was granted warrants against defaulters. One man who had failed to carry out his customary six days highway work in 1762 was obliged (or rather he 'agreed') to perform 12 days the subsequent year.[51]

The Weaknesses of Local Officers

The weakest link in the administration of the law was always the local officials, under pressure not to report offences, or facing too many temptations to misconduct. One Sunderland constable, Matthew Cook, accused of defrauding a workman of £1 15s, attracted Tew's comment that 'there is not a greater villain than

---

49 W.E. Tate, *The Parish Chest: a Study of the Records of Parochial Administration in England*, 3rd edition (Cambridge, 1969), p. 193.

50 Compare Tew's cases in the Notebook, May 31st 1763 and June 7th 1756 (bastardy), Febuary 12th 1760 and April 23rd 1761 (idiocy), August 9th 1753 and September 4th 1764 (removals), among many others.

51 Notebook, January 14th 1757 and July 11th 1763.

Cook'. More predictably, a churchwarden of Chester-le-Street was accused of having fathered a bastard child. Other officials needed Tew's suppport: he swore in the bread-weighers and 'inspectors into meal' of South Shields, probably because the local justices who were in charge in the parish were not actually resident there. Salt officers reported untaxed salt to him and asked for warrants against offenders. Window tax collectors needed protection from assault when going about their duties. It is possible that local officials were dutiful but not particularly well educated: certainly one of Boldon's overseers (and churchwardens) signed his name with a mark throughout his service.[52]

Employment Conditions

The supervision of contracts of employment of servants and apprentices provided all local magistrates in the eighteenth century with a great deal of troublesome business. The customary role of justices in ensuring that masters and their servants or apprentices behaved appropriately to each other remained important despite the increasing scale of industrial enterprises. One recurrent grievance against employers was the non-payment of wages, or provision of sufficient food: Tew was continually trying to enforce their proper behaviour in this regard. Some masters kept the clothes and personal property of their servants when they left. Others refused to teach their apprentices the trade to which they had been recruited. Justices had particular responsibility for seeing that employees kept to their work, and that their employers did not abuse them. Abuse of apprentices could be dealt with by a lone justice acting against the employers; by contrast, orders to imprison servants or apprentices for idleness or misbehaviour, or to annul the contract of employment or apprenticeship, usually required two justices.[53] Boldon was a rural area, and many farms in the north east retained living-in servants. Moreover, many non-agricultural businesses were just as small as a family farm. Only in the mines in the middle of the eight-

52 Notebook, August 11th 1760 (Cook), November 6th 1755 (churchwarden), July 14th 1761 (window tax); DRO, EP/Bo 42, p. 52 (John Heath overseer, 1751, who signs with a mark, and who also occurs in PRO DURH 17/7, for the homicide of John Garth, when he fled from justice initially. This incident is referred to in the Notebook on September 4th and 7th 1751).

53 Burn, *The Justice of the Peace*, vol. 1, pp. 63, 76–7; vol. 3, pp. 241, 260 for servants.

eenth century were there large workforces, but here Tew treated pitmen in the same way as runaway apprentices, forcing workers to return to their employers. There are several instances of men who had left their service in the mines belonging to John Blackett being ordered back to work. Here too, wages were sometimes an issue of contention, as money allocated to pay subordinates was not always passed on.[54]

Conflicts and Reputations

Much of the routine business in the notebook centres on forms of violence, both communal and domestic, and personal attacks, involving physical assault and, in some instances, slanderous attacks on the reputations of neighbours. Reputation was a valuable personal quality, worth defending because difficult to restore if lost. Much work has been done on the earlier period when church courts, in providing the main outlet for slander cases, allowed the aggrieved to act against their detractors and demand public apologies in the form of penances. The notebook confirms that some of this business was transferred to the secular authorities after 1700. Yet the published justices' handbooks were unclear whether such matters as slander or scandalous words were appropriate business for local magistrates.[55] Nevertheless, attempts to destroy individuals' 'name and fame' through rumours of sexual infidelity, and even one accusation of witchcraft (but the parties were 'both scolds and fools'), appear as complaints made to Tew: significantly, the majority, as in the church courts, were slanders against women, often made by other women. Some men, even so, were anxious to defend their reputations, particularly if, as a consequence, their business was threatened. One man complained of a false rumour that he had venereal disease which was deterring his customers

54 Notebook, June 9th and July 27th 1762; similarly August 26th 1757 (an order to pitmen working for Nicholas Lambton Esq.), January 22nd 1763 (money not passed on). See A. Kussmaul, *Servants in Husbandry in Early Modern England* (Cambridge, 1981), and P. Rushton, '"The Matter in Variance": Adolescents and Domestic Conflict in the Pre-Industrial Economy of Northeast England, 1600–1800', *Journal of Social History*, 25 (1), 1991, pp. 89–107.

55 J.A. Sharpe, *Defamation and Sexual Slanders in Early Modern England: the Church Courts at York*, Borthwick Papers 58 (York, 1980); P. Rushton, 'Women, Witchcraft and Slander in Early Modern England: Cases from the Church Courts of Durham, 1560–1675', *Northern History*, 18, 1982, pp. 116–32; Burn, *The Justice of the Peace*, vol. 3, p. 295.

from buying his milk and butter. In other types of cases too, Tew demonstrated an interest in the previously established reputations of those before him. For example, he noted in a bastardy case that the woman had reputedly been acquitted of theft at the quarter sessions a couple of years before.[56] Moreover, with his ready assumptions about people's reputation expressed in blunt phrases such as 'they are common strumpets', or 'bad impudent people', Tew followed the contemporary culture of relating credibility to public character. When a complainant turned out to be untrustworthy, he concluded that the accusation, however serious, even rape, must fall.

Reputation also figured in the domestic affairs which are reported in the notebook. Rumours of wives' infidelity or sexual deviance were perceived as undermining their relationships with their husbands, and the couples complained to Tew to restore their good name. Other couples needed no outside encouragement to fall out with one another, for several wives accused their husbands of violence and desertion. The latter seemingly evoked a swifter or more severe response, because of the Poor Law costs of families without a male wage, but some of the reported incidents of domestic violence also needed resolution. James Weddal, a South Shields boatman, was accused of 'beating, and chaining down to a log for more than two hours, Dorothy his wife, when naked, and threatening her life'. Tew subsequently recorded that Weddal had 'gone into the King's service' in the navy, presumably regarding the separation of the couple as some kind of solution to a case which had run through his notebook for many months previously.[57] The marital disputes such as this in the notebook reflect interestingly on the limits of public tolerance of private domestic abuse. Husbands guilty of 'cruel usage' of their wives, or who threatened to kill them were liable to be summoned to answer for their behaviour.

Conclusion

The processes of justice that emerge from sources such as Tew's notebook are therefore a distinctive mixture of the formal and the

---

56 Notebook, June 7th 1762 (witchcraft), September 22nd 1760 (venereal disease), June 10th 1762 (Elisabeth Marshall, who at the assizes of 1761 was found guilty of a lesser charge and branded: PRO, DURH 16/1).

57 Notebook, May 6th and 17th, October 29th and 31st 1763 (Weddal).

informal. Within the confines of the law, solutions were sometimes imposed, sometimes openly negotiated, and at other times left to develop without much official approval. That a magistrate such as Tew was kept so busy is a tribute to the way that the law had become integrated into so many aspects of people's lives in the early modern period. Generally, however, the evidence of this notebook points to the way that early modern communities solved their problems through semi-private dealings before their local justices rather than by formal prosecutions in the courts. The purpose of 'going to law' was not to achieve a conviction so much as to settle the personal disputes between individuals by restoring their broken social relations – in effect, ensuring a return to the customary social behaviour on which communal life depended.[58]

EDITORIAL METHOD

The notebook is 15 cms (6 inches) wide, 24.5cms (9.75 inches) high, and about 2 cms (0.75 inch) thick. It is roughly bound and has had metal clasps at one time; on the spine is written 'Notes of a Revd. J.P.', with '1750' on the front cover and '1750' on the back cover. It was bought at auction at Sotheby's by Durham Record Office, with the assistance of the Victoria and Albert Museum, on 27th January 1984.

Tew's notebook is written in ink, with each entry separated from the next by a horizontal line. The entries usually are dated with the day of the month, giving the type of warrant, the names of the plaintiff and defendant, and, usually, an outcome. The warrants are initially spelled out clearly – general or special – but become increasingly abbreviated and eventually reduced to simple phrases such as 'G. G. warrt.'. Only the rarer search warrants or summonses remain clearly elaborated and need no expansion. The outcomes of cases are given alongside or after the entries, usually briefly in one or two words. For a few entries Tew used a capital 'A' to indicate 'Agreed'. All shortened expres-

58 See J.A. Sharpe, '"Such Disagreement betwyx Neighbours": Litigation and Human Relations in Early Modern England', in J. Bossy (ed.), *Disputes and Settlements: Law and Human Relations in the West* (Cambridge, 1983), pp. 167–87; R.B. Shoemaker, *Prosecution and Punishment: Petty Crime and the Law in London and Rural Middlesex, c.1660–1725* (Cambridge, 1991).

sions have been expanded for clarity, as have the most obvious abbreviations.

The general style, including spelling and use of abbreviations, is inconsistent. In this edition capitalization has been modernized, and some punctuation, such as apostrophes and commas, has been added, for the sake of readability. The original spelling of names of persons, including the common spelling 'Elisabeth', and other words, has been retained; some initials in names have been left, where their expansion is unclear. Place-names have been expanded, so that, for example, 'Sunderland' is printed consistently in place of Tew's own Sunderland, Sunderl^{d}, Sund^{d}, and Sun^{d} - and 'Monk Wearmouth' in place of his Monk Wearmouth, M. Wearmouth and M. Wearmth. Idiosyncratic spellings have not been modernized; where Tew uses Jarro and Westo instead of Jarrow and Westoe, these forms have been kept in the transcription. The punctuation of N.B. (which Tew employs frequently) is standardized throughout.

The document is paginated for the first 58 pages until almost the end of 1757, but otherwise is unstructured. There are three types of pencil markings on top of the ink. One, which may be near contemporary, is in black or graphite pencil, usually involving the complete striking through of whole entries. The others, in blue and red, seem to highlight interesting issues or individuals, and are most probably the work of a nineteenth-century owner. Some indication of these have been given in the footnotes.

Tew coded his cases according to two systems, one up to the end of October 1757, the other from then on. The first system comprised short strokes through the line above each entry, mostly running through the line, but sometimes sitting on the line. Some entries are coded with a small circle, or 'o'. Even though the significance of these symbols has not been discovered, they have been systematically recorded in this edition after each entry in italics within square brackets; strokes through the line are counted as whole strokes, and those only on top of the line as half strokes. Though he kept this system of strokes for some uses after November 1757 (about the same point where the pagination ceases), he switched his normal coding to a system of small letters such as 'o', 's', 'ss' or 'sm', placed at the end of each entry. These seem to bear little relation to the types of cases or their resolution. Many letters and orders are finished with 'o', and many warrants with 'sm' (one for each name if several people are listed). All we can say from extensive research, widespread consultation with scholarly colleagues, and advice from many quarters, is that these usages are not a variety of the shorthands (such as that used by Bishop Chandler's office) or ciphers customary in the eighteenth century, and seem to have no parallel in any other published notebook kept by a justice of the peace.

EDITORIAL CONVENTIONS

1755	text underlined in Tew's hand.
[*inserted*, word]	text inserted in Tew's hand by interlineation or substitution.
[*deleted*, word]	text deleted in Tew's hand.
[*margin*, text]	text Tew squeezed to the left of the main textual field in the original MS.
[*sic*]	editorial comment.
Λ<greed>	under defined text expanded by the editors.
R<*e*>y	badly written text.

THE NOTEBOOK

[*Inside the front cover*]
Mem[d]. Thomas Tinmouth of South Shields a general *informer*.
Rebecca Delaval – quite infamous.
Elisabeth Waugh wife of [*blank*] Waugh of Shields taylor is a notorious scold and impudent woman.[1]
2. About the character of Rebecca Williamson *aged 18* at Monk Wearmouth and Susanna Crow wife of Robert Crow trimmer.[2] *N.B.* Both extremely bad – one a common woman and one a *fortuneteller*.[3]

[*On the flyleaf*]
Peter Ovington Bailif of Sunderland.[4]

[*page*] 1
An account of business since I acted as Justice of Peace.

Mem. I gave an order for erecting stocks and pinfold in West Boldon.[5]

1750 November 16th *James Colvin* weaver swore the peace against *Ralph Atkinson* of East Boldon – made them friends and James Colvin released on the 19th.

---

1 Both 'notorious scold' and 'impudent woman' are underlined in red pencil.
2 See March 17th 1759 for Susanna and Robert Crow.
3 Both 'common' and '*fortuneteller*' are underlined in red pencil. Below these entries in Tew's hand, a nineteenth century hand has inserted 'Nearly the same 100 years ago' (in pencil) and 'Supposed to be the notes of The Reverend Edmund Tew who was Rector of Boldon from 1735 to 1770' (in ink).
4 Below this, which is in Tew's hand, later writer(s) have inserted 'Edmund Tew, Rector of Boldon from 1735 to 1770' (in pencil), 'purchased at Gateshead for 1/6' (in black ink) and 'John Kidson, Sunderland' (in purple ink). The name 'Gavin Milburn' in Gothic lettering is added with a stamp, using black ink, in the top right corner of the page.
5 The word 'stocks' is underlined in red pencil.

December 13th Granted a warrant for the *constable* or overseer of *Barnston* in Washington Parish to relieve Robert Bayster wife and 3 children (Robert Bayster having been ill for nine weeks) or to show cause, why he does not – relieved with 2s per week.

December 31st Granted a summons warrant for Simon Dixon and Elizabeth Watson of South Shields to appear before me (or any other Justice) to answer to the complaint of Joseph Cowper for stealing a sack etc. – Agreed.[6]

January 22nd[7] Granted a summons warrant for John Storey mariner of Monk Wearmouth Shore to appear before me to answer the complaint of Thomas Hylton, for threatening to have his life and skin. Agreed.

February 3rd Granted a search warrant to John Bell Farmer at Suddick[8] upon the oath of his servant Joseph Dodd that he had lost 2 sows, which were almost fat, on Friday last. [*1 stroke*]

February 12th Granted a pass to Katherine Hyme wife of Richard Hyme grenadiar to Canterbury within one month. Note: she afterwards fell in labour at East Boldon.

17th Committed Robert Wilson of Sunderland mariner to Durham goal for felony upon his own confession and proof, and bound over Thomas Richardson mariner in £40 penalty to prosecute.

Mem. Refused to take the oath of [*blank*] Carr wife of Thomas Carr of Monk Wearmouth against her husband for ill usage.

February 20th Granted a summons warrant against Anthony Reay joyner of South Shields upon the oath of Edward Grey joyner of ditto, that he stole an half inch hollow and [*inserted,* half inch] round plane from him. To appear before me or other Justice. [*1 stroke; margin,* A<greed>]

---

6 The word 'Agreed' is underlined in red pencil.

7 This is following the official old style of dating, which until 1752 commenced the year on 25th March.

8 I.e. Southwick.

February 25th Gave a summons warrant against Philip Weightman mariner of South Shields for taking out of Robert Wilson's stable of ditto a mare and happing of John Leighton's of Fulwell blacksmith. Before me. [*margin,* Not found]

[*page*] 2 *1750*[9]

March 5th Granted warrant to bring Elizabeth Hayward hired servant of Joseph Yellowly of Hylton for refusing to work – Before me. [*margin,* (Agreed)]

11th Gave a pass to Katherine Hyme and infant to go to Canterbury in ten weeks' time to her husband Richard Hyme, who is quartered there and in Lord Ancram's Regiment.

15th Granted a warrant of summons for Thomas Carr butcher of Shields for firing six rods of hedge belonging to Richard Fawel of Waresly in Jarrow parish. [*margin, Agreed* [*underlined*]; *to the right,* Before me]

22nd Convicted John Garth of Boldon mason of drunkenness upon the oath of William Rowland and fined him 5s: but we gave back 2s 6d to the wife.

23rd Signed a church rate for the parish of Sunderland.[10]

23rd Granted a warrant against William Coverdale of the ship Parnassus for cruelly using and wounding in the head Joseph Bell of the said ship – before me, or another. [*margin,* Not found]

1751[11]

25th Allowed [*blank*] Barkas of Jarrow servant to be turned of<f> by his master, for leaving him 3 times, and abridged the servant of near six weeks' wages.

---

9 This was 1751 by modern reckoning; see note 7 above.

10 Two justices had the duty of consenting to a rate assessment, 'by way of form', but the churchwardens and overseers had the power of setting it: R. Burn, *The Justice of the Peace and Parish Officer*, 6th edition (London, 1758), vol. 3, p. 112.

11 I.e. dating the beginning of the year from 25th March.

28th Grace Lundy singlewoman of Sunderland swore this day her bastard child to James Collender of the same.

30th Thomas Price (by a warrant from Mr Lambe) apprentice to Mr Cockerill of South Shields was brought before me for disobedience to his master, and reprimanded, the master not being present, to make full proof, but only the head servant.[12]

April 1st Granted a warrant to Thomas Alder overseer of Sunderland to take up the above James Collender for getting a bastard child – before any Justice. Note: He married her. [$2\frac{1}{2}$ *strokes; margin,* A<greed>]

4th Granted search warrant upon oath of Phillis Longstaff of Monk Wearmouth having lost cotton gown etc. against Alice Hall, Mary Bruce and others of ill fame only.

[*page*] 3 *1751*

April 10th 1751 Granted warrant upon oath of John Musgrave blacksmith of South Shields against William Shepherd skipper of the same, for bruising and giving <a> black eye to the said John Musgrave. [$1\frac{1}{2}$ *strokes; margin,* A<greed>]

Mem. Refused a warrant to Anthony Reay carpenter of ditto for a man's calling his wife whore etc., as I did also yesterday to a landlady at Cleedon, and another landlady of South Shields.

12th Granted warrant upon oath of Mary Hathaway [*inserted,* Haddock] widow of South Shields against John Lee, alias Leigh [*inserted,* watchman] of ditto for assaulting and beating and using her with great imodesty on the 8th instant, without the least pro-

12 Reverend William Lambe, Durham born, and vicar of Gateshead 1733–69, was a very active magistrate, and frequently on the bench at the quarter sessions; DRO, Q/S/OB 10-12. He is first recorded on the commission of the peace in 1737, PRO, C192/2, part 1. He was notorious in the history of Gateshead for pulling down the cottages of the tenants of King James's Hospital and ejecting them; J. Foster (ed.), *Alumni Oxonienses: the Members of the University of Oxford* (Nendeln, Liechtenstein, 1968), vol. 3, p. 811; F.W.D. Manders, *A History of Gateshead* (Gateshead, 1973), pp. 219–20.

vocation (Mem. They are both persons of bad character).[13] [*margin*, Acquitted]

19th Granted warrant upon oath of William Taylor of Westo joyner against Anthony Reay of South Shields joyner for stealing the tools of the said Taylor (Note: this is the 2nd information against Anthony Reay).
Agreed. Special. [*1 stroke; margin*, A<greed>]

23rd Refused a warrant against widow Raby, publican of Shoreside for opprobrious words etc. against Alexander Knox's [*inserted*, trimmer] wife, 2 very touchy people.

May 14th Wrote to John Thwaits skipper of Shoreside for threatening the wife of [*blank*]

28th Granted warrant upon oath of John Smith labourer of Bishop Wearmouth against Thomas Duncan of the same parish for his detaining his shovel, and threatening and abusing the said Smith and his wife. General. [*1 stroke; margin*, A<greed>]

June 1st Granted warrant against William Middleton of Westo maltmaker upon oath of Ann Bate wife of William Bate higler of the same place for bruising in her secret parts and arm, disclosing them to several persons and threatening her life. Special.[14] [$2\frac{1}{2}$ *strokes; margin*, Agreed]

6th Granted warrant against John Dixon apprentice to Captain George Stephenson for absenting himself from his master's service etc. General. [*margin*, Agreed]

6th Granted warrant against Isable the wife of John Young taylor upon complaint of Anthony Wall barber of South Shields for threatening to kill and maim the same Wall.
(Note: Anthony Wall is a very bad man, and son-in-law to Mary Haddock).[15] [*margin*, Agreed; *to the right*, General]

---

13 Entry crossed through in black pencil.
14 Entry crossed through in black and red pencil; two red pencil strokes in left margin.
15 Entry crossed through in black pencil.

[*page*] 4 *1751*

June 8th 1751 Granted general warrant against Ralph Purvis cobleman of Shields upon oath of John Wilkie mariner of the same for threatening to beat out his brains. [$2\frac{1}{2}$ *strokes; margin,* A<greed>]

13th Sent a letter to Mr Francis Hawke of Shields for detaining wages due to old Edward Hunter of the same place.

14th Granted general warrant against Richard Wilkinson weaver of Sunderland upon complaint of Mary Winny for beating and abusing her and detaining her wages. *Mem.* After committment ordered for not finding sureties, Richard Wilkinson paid all charges. [$2\frac{1}{2}$ *strokes; margin,* A<greed>]

17th Granted general warrant against Jane Medcalf servant to Edward Softley of Boldon for absenting herself from his service.

24th Granted general warrant against John, Isabella, Jane and Mary Cornforth of the parish of Sunderland upon oath of Charles Champerley mariner and alehouse keeper, for beating, threatening and cutting his hand etc. [$2\frac{1}{2}$ *strokes; margin,* A<greed>]

Granted general warrant against Isable Ekins wife of David Ekins labourer of Sunderland for assaulting and beating Mary Flockton baker of the same. [*margin,* A<greed>]

26th Granted general warrant against Elizabeth Taylor servant to Jeremiah and Dorothy Abbs of Monk Wearmouth for absenting herself from her service, with an order to bring Thomas Forster taylor her father-in-law for harbouring her. (Allowed the deposition and ordered her to return to her servitude).[16] [$2\frac{1}{2}$ *strokes*]

---

16 The younger Jeremiah Abbs was tried in 1756, and acquitted, of drinking the Pretender's health and wishing damnation to King George; PRO, SP 36/136/1. This is probably his father, who was on the grand jury at the quarter sessions in 1749, DRO, Q/S/OB 10, p. 199. Entry crossed through in black pencil; red pencil stroke in left margin.

29th Granted general warrant against Benjamin Nicholson and a person unknown (a tall young man) for riotously assaulting, breaking windows, and abusing J. Paul and Samuel Harvey alehousekeepers and their wives etc. [$2\frac{1}{2}$ *strokes; margin,* Not found]

July 3rd Granted general warrant against Thomas Henderson apprentice to Thomas Young of Boldon for running away from his servitude.

5th Granted special warrant against Isable wife of George Holmes of Shields brickmaker for assaulting, and beating, and throwing a pail of water upon Hannah Garret servant of Thomas Gibson of ditto. Agreed. [$2\frac{1}{2}$ *strokes; margin,* A<greed>]

[*page*] 5 *1751*

July 16th Granted general warrant against William Dicks mariner of Monk Wearmouth Shore upon oath of [*inserted,* Captain] Edward Hutchinson of ditto, for assaulting and bruising his wife and breaking his windows. Agreed the matter betwixt them upon William Dicks paying bill and charges 14s 9d. [$2\frac{1}{2}$ *strokes*]

27th Granted general warrant against Elizabeth Young servant to Edward Watson saltmaker in Shields for leaving her service. [*1 stroke; margin,* A<greed>]

August 5th Elizabeth Curry singlewoman of Sunderland swore this day her bastard child to Thomas Ridley master and mariner of the same on the 21st or 22nd December last. Note: he gave bond to the parish.[17] [$2\frac{1}{2}$ *strokes; margin,* A<greed>]

8th Granted general warrant against Mary Paul of Shields for assaulting and bruising Elizabeth [*inserted,* her own sister] wife of Bernard Lunbury of ditto and for breaking her household goods. N.B. They are both bad women and keep bad houses. [$2\frac{1}{2}$ *strokes; margin,* Not found]

17 Entry crossed through in black pencil.

14th Granted general warrant against Robert Lawson brickmaker of Shields for beating and threatening William Fenwick brickmaker of the same. [*1 stroke; margin*, Agreed]

21st Granted general warrant against Thomas Robson, William Fenwick and Elizabeth his wife, Alexander Fenwick and Thomas Cutter [*inserted*, all brickmakers at Shields] for assaulting and knocking down and wounding James Cockburn glasshouse-man of Shields on Saturday night the 17th instant. [$2\frac{1}{2}$ *strokes; margin*, A<greed>]

22nd Convicted Laurence Ogle of Shields baker for selling bread (contrary to the Assize) 8 ounces deficient at 5s per oz, upon the oath of Thomas Robinson of Shields mariner, but made up all for Laurence Ogle for 18s 6d to informer etc.[18] [$4\frac{1}{2}$ *strokes*]

24th Granted general warrant against Margaret wife of Isaac Wardel roper of Sunderland, for beating and threatening to have the life of Elizabeth Elwick, upon oath of her husband William Elwick, and that she is unable to attend in person. N.B. Margaret Wardel is supposed to have 2 husbands.[19] [$2\frac{1}{2}$ *strokes; margin*, Not found]

[*page*] 6 *1751*

August 26th Heard the charge of theft against Thomas Clarke of East Boldon taylor and made up the affair betwixt him and the accuser, a servantmaid to George Man upon her paying 6s 10d. [$2\frac{1}{2}$ *strokes*]

Granted general warrant against Thomas Thompson hired servant to Anthony Tinmouth fisherman of Shields for not entering into his service according to bargain and earnest. [*1 stroke; margin*, Agreed]

31st Granted general warrant against Joseph <Gru>nwell, Joseph Hardy, Samuel Watson butchers of Sunderland for giving in sure-

---

18 Entry crossed through in black pencil; one red pencil stroke in left margin.
19 Entry crossed through in black pencil.

ties of the peace upon the oath of Christopher Eylls butcher [*inserted*, of Sunderland] whom they assaulted – *N.B.* Christopher Eylls is a quarrelsome man.[20] [$2\frac{1}{2}$ *strokes; margin*, Agreed]

Granted general warrant against Edward Atkinson of Fulwell, horsebreaker and alehousekeeper for assaulting and striking with his whip 3 times Francis Thompson shopkeeper of Monk Wearmouth Shoreside. Agreed. [$2\frac{1}{2}$ *strokes*]

September 2nd Granted general warrant against John Philip apprentice to James Forrest of Shields fisherman for leaving his service. [*1 stroke; margin*, Agreed]

4th Granted warrant for summons and after hearing I punished William Waster of East Boldon alehousekeeper 10s for suffering tipling in his house and took away his licence for 3 years, after the death of John Garth.[21] [$2\frac{1}{2}$ *strokes*]

Convicted also Thomas Atkinson alehousekeeper of ditto for the same crime [inserted, and intended to have] remitted him 5s out of the 10s but he was impudent.[22] [*1 stroke*]

Convicted also of drunkenness, Thomas Wood, George Wood, William Brown, Peter Marshall, William Tweddale, William Hallowell, and John Rippon of drunkenness and levyed 5s upon each of them, and distributed the money to the poor of the parish. [*7 strokes*]

7th Granted general warrant against John Rippon mason of Boldon for being concerned in the affray at Wastal's house and for incouraging and abetting John Heath in beating John Garth, to find sureties for the good behaviour.[23] [*2 or perhaps* $2\frac{1}{2}$ *strokes*]

---

20 Entry crossed through in black pencil.

21 Entry crossed through in black pencil; one red pencil stroke in left margin.

22 Entry crossed through in black pencil.

23 PRO, DURH 17/7, 6 September 1751, records the depositions taken before William Peverell in the case of the death of John Garth, assaulted by John Heath in an affray after drinking at William Waistell's illegal alehouse. The issue was a debt owed by Garth to Heath. The case never came to court. William Waistell appears in this Notebook in 1751 and 1752, pursued by Tew under alehouse legislation.

[*page*] *7 1751*

William Brown carpenter, Robert Matthew and Robert Elliott all entered into recognizance, Brown in £40 and Matthew and Elliott in £20 a peice for Brown's appearance at the next Assizes for Durham.[24] [$2\frac{1}{2}$ *strokes*]

[*There are no entries for October 1751 – March 1752.*]

April 1st 1752 Wrote a letter to Ralph Thompson of Shields for a debt of 4s 6d at the request of old Edward Hunter of [*inserted,* ditto] (who appears a very troublesome fellow, and maddish).[25]

11th Wrote to Mr Green attorney in Sunderland upon complaint of Thomas Carre of Monk Wearmouth Shore, horse-letter, that he had knocked him down etc. for asking only for horse hire and I saw his head was then bloody.[26]

13th Granted general warrant against the above John Green upon oath of the said Thomas Carre.[27] [$2\frac{1}{2}$ *strokes*]

13th Granted general warrant against the above John Green upon oath of Jane Carr of Sunderland Pans, for breaking head, and giving her many visible bruises on the eye, arm, back etc. for asking him for a debt due to her.[28] [$2\frac{1}{2}$ *strokes*]

Mem: On the 13th April 1752 John Green attorney at law of Sunderland in £20 and Richard Matthew and Joseph Cooper in £10 each, entered into recognizance, that the said John Green appear

---

24 There is no record of William Brown's appearance at the assizes.

25 Entry crossed through in black pencil; two red pencil strokes in left margin; 'fellow and maddish' underlined in red pencil.

26 John Green, attorney, made numerous appearances at the quarter sessions, including this case, for which he was fined 1s, and also £5 for assaulting magistrate George Baker of Elemore Hall, and sentenced to remain in jail until it was paid: DRO, Q/S/OB 10, pp. 323–5 and 332. Entry crossed through in black pencil; two red pencil strokes in left margin; 'attorney' underlined in red pencil.

27 Entry crossed through in black pencil; one red pencil stroke in left margin; 'John Green' underlined in red pencil.

28 Entry crossed through in black pencil; one red pencil stroke in left margin.

at the next quarter sessions of the peace at Durham to answer for an assault and battery at the prosecution of Thomas Carre.[29]

Mem. On ditto, the above three entered also into recognizance as above, that John Green should appear as above to answer above at the prosecution of Jane Carr. *Mem.* Jane Carr released on the 16th April.

17th April Granted special warrant against John Harkas for refusing to serve his master John Walker mason of South Shields according to written agreement. Agreed. [*1 stroke*]

[*page*] 8 *1752*

April 20th 1752 Granted general warrant against Simon Miller taylor of South Shields for refusing to pay 4s 11d for wages due to Walter Elliot. [*1 stroke*]

May 1st Granted special warrant against William Brown hired servant of George Man of Monk Wearmouth for refusing to serve out his time. [*circle*]

8th Granted special warrant against Richard Gardiner alehousekeeper at Sunderland for refusing to give up a silver can value £3 10s 0d the property of James Angus blacksmith of Jarro, which was stolen out of his house April 20th last. *Note.* James Hewit silversmith of Sunderland bought the handle of the said can at 2s 6d when bruised and battered of one Mary Holland – This is the 2nd time of his buying stolen goods. 2: his character indiff<erent>.[30] [$2\frac{1}{2}$ *strokes*]

10th Granted special warrant against Elizabeth Atkinson a hired servant to Reverend Mr Gooday for running away from her service. Agreed.[31]

---

29 'Mem:', 'John Green attorney', and 'next quarter sessions' underlined in red pencil.

30 Entry crossed through in black pencil; one red pencil stroke in left margin.

31 Reverend Thomas Gooday of Monkwearmouth, 1742–68, was author of *The Complaint in the Day of Desertion*: R. Surtees, *The History and Antiquities of the County Palatine of Durham etc.* (London, 1820), vol. 2, p. 12.

13th Sent a warrant of distraint against the above Simon Miller of Shields for the debt of 4s 11d and charges 8s, in all 12s 11d for which warrant I paid Mr Huntley 2s.[32]

18th Issued out a summons warrant against Robert Pruddo and William Wastal of East Boldon for keeping an alehouse, without licenses, and to appear and show cause why they should not be punished 20s each.[33]

19th They appeared and showing no cause, William Wastal confessing and promising to pay the 20s, I granted no distress warrant against him, but I granted warrant of distress against Robert Pruddo who confessed likewise, but pretended he had not to pay.[34]

25th Granted special warrant against John Rutherford mariner of Monk Wearmouth parish for threatening the life of George Moor of East Boldon and disobeying his lawful commands etc. Agreed.

[*page*] 9 *1752*

Mem. On the 25th of May 1752 having convicted William Wastal and Robert Pruddo for keeping alehouses without licences, the said Wastal and Pruddo paid 20s each into the hands of Anthony Snowball constable which was paid by him to the churchwarden of Boldon and distributed equally to the poor of the said parish.[35]

June 1st Granted special warrant against John Swan glassblower of Shields for throwing <a> red hot pipe and bottle against Thomas Betson glassman of the same and burning his neck. Agreed.[36] [$2\frac{1}{2}$ *strokes*]

Granted special warrant against William Lazenby boat-builder of Shields for wilfully pushing down Joyce (the wife of John Wilkie mariner) a steep bank, by the fall whereof, she is much hurt and

32 Two red pencil strokes in left margin.
33 Two red pencil strokes in left margin.
34 Entry crossed through in black pencil; one red pencil stroke in left margin.
35 Entry crossed through in black pencil; two red pencil strokes in left margin.
36 Entry crossed through in black pencil.

in danger of miscarriage, etc., upon the oaths of the said John and William Atkinson of South Shields. [*partly deleted,* Agreed afterwards.][37] [$2\frac{1}{2}$ *strokes*]

Mem. On June 2nd 1752 the above William Lazenby in £40, William Common [*inserted,* schoolmaster] in £20, and John Somerson mariner in £20, entered into recognizance etc., released 3s.4d. [3 *strokes and the figure* 4]

June 4th Wrote a letter to Mr Thomas Ayres shipbuilder in Sunderland upon 8 of his apprentices complaining of want of victuals etc. Agreed.

26th Granted special warrant against Nathaniel Dunbar of Shields shoemaker for assaulting and beating Philip Chilton shoemaker of the same place (but late of Chester-le-Street), and for putting him in fear of his life by blows and menaces. [$2\frac{1}{2}$ *strokes*]

[*page*] 10 *1752*

June 29th Granted special warrant against Martha Charlton of Suddick[38] spinster for feloniously taking coals from Suddick glass-house key, the property of John Bell of Monk Wearmouth. Agreed. [*1 stroke*]

July 3rd Granted special warrant against John Park apprentice to John Errington barber of Monk Wearmouth Shore for leaving his service. Note: the master is a notorious drunkard and frantick. [*1 stroke; margin,* Agreed]

9th Granted special warrant against Adam [*blank*] hired servant to Alice Heath widdow of Monk Wearmouth parish for leaving his service. [*margin,* Agreed]

13th Received information by William Rowland of Boldon against William Matthew tanner of ditto for being drunk and abusing him and family etc. on the 9th instant.

37 Three red pencil strokes in left margin, which are themeselves crossed through in black pencil.

38 I.e. Southwick.

14th Sent a summons warrant to Matthew by A. Snowball constable and upon his coming before me and alledging nothing material, I convicted him in the penalty of 5s and issued out a warrant of distraint accordingly. N.B. I returned the conviction to the quarter sessions.

20th Granted special warrant against Elinor Brown, Christiana Brown, Charles Hardy and Barbara Newton for abusing the good name and fame of James and Jane Zechariah, all of the parish of Monk Wearmouth, and charging them with a robbery.[39] [2½ *strokes; margin,* Dismissed]

Granted special warrant against Jacob Pennyman skipper for abusing the good name and fame of John Garry (both of Sunderland) and for charging the said Garry with picking his pocket of 7s 6d.
N.B. Jacob Pennyman is of bad character.[40] [*1 stroke; margin,* Agreed]

August 3rd Granted special warrant against Nathaniel Tate master and mariner of Sunderland for detaining the wages of Sarah Leng [*inserted,* 8s 9d] and Mary Robinson [*inserted,* 4s 2d]. [*margin,* He paid them]

8th Granted special warrant against Joseph Snowdon skipper of Sunderland for beating and breaking out a tooth of Anne the wife of John Donkin keelman of the same place. [2½ *strokes*]

[*page*] 11 *1752*

August 12th Granted special warrant against Matthew Robson barber and Elizabeth his wife of Sunderland for assaulting and beating Elizabeth Bulman wife of James Bulman and Hannah their daughter. [2½ *strokes; margin,* Agreed]

---

39 One red pencil stroke in left margin, itself crossed through in black pencil.

40 Two red pencil strokes in left margin, themselves crossed through in black pencil.

Jane Burton widow of Llinlithgow swore this day (the 12th of August 1752) a bastard child against William Hardy of Sunderland about the 2nd week in May.

17th Bound over John Errington barber of Monk Wearmouth Shore for abusing his apprentice John Park. [*margin*, Parted at the sessions]

19th Granted general warrant against Thomas Stephenson master and mariner (of Whitby) if found in our county, for detaining the wages of Richard Johnson his apprentice, being £4 11s 0d.

[*There are no entries for September 1752 – April 1753.*]

1753

May 21st 1753 Summoned William Wastal of East Boldon to inquire why he kept an alehouse without a licence, and upon his confession convicted him in the penalty of 20s, which were distributed by the churchwarden William Atkinson to the poor of Boldon.[41]

May 23rd 1753 Granted special warrant against Ralph Burfield [*inserted*, to John [*blank*]] master and mariner for detaining the wages of William Stafford. Agreed, it being a vexacious complaint and made Stafford pay the charges.

[*There are no entries for June – July 1753.*]

August 9th 1753 Granted a pass to Ralph Wilkinson a lame mason, his wife and 2 children to go from hence to the town of Birmingham to the parish of St. Thomas, being the sworn place of their settlement.

[*page*] 12 *1753*

August 15th Granted general warrant upon oath of Archibald Sympson sawyer of Sunderland against George and George

41 Entry crossed through in black pencil.

Hodge [*sic*] of the same for beating and abusing the wife of the said Archibald, who has miscarryed and in danger of death. Note: They agreed. [$2\frac{1}{2}$ *strokes*]

August 23rd Granted general warrant to Selby Pearson farmer of Wooler in the county of Northumberland against William Brown his hired servant for departing from his service before expiration. [*1 stroke; margin,* Agreed to pay a quarter's wages]

28th Granted special warrant upon oath of Margaret Grey wife of Charles Grey pilot of South Shields [*inserted,* against J. Lukeham carpenter of South Shields] for beating and bruising her. [$2\frac{1}{2}$ *strokes; margin,* Agreed]

Convicted a pedlar upon information of Mr Bainbridge of Whitburn, and mitigated the fine to £3; £1 10s 0d to the informer, and £1 10s 0d to Whitburn parish.[42]

29th Granted special warrant against Henry Taylor sail-maker and baker [*inserted,* of Sunderland] upon complaint of his apprentice Ralph Harrison by his father, for cruelly beating and bruising him. [$2\frac{1}{2}$ *strokes*]

September 3rd Granted special warrant against Thomas Jeffreson servant of Robert Rochester of South Shields skipper for leaving his service. [*1 stroke*]

Granted special warrant against Andrew Alexander of Shields fisherman for detaining 5s 10d wages due to James Armstrong. [*1 stroke; margin,* Ordered 3s]

Granted special warrant against George Crofton of Jarro for detaining 6s wages due to George Robertson [*1 stroke; margin,* N.B. George Crofton paid wages and charges]

[*page*] 13 *1753*

September 18th Granted special warrant against Simon [*blank*]

---

42 One red pencil stroke in left margin; 'pedlar' underlined in red pencil.

ship-carpenter of Shields for assaulting and threatening Mr [*blank*] Blagdon blacksmith of ditto. [$2\frac{1}{2}$ *strokes*]

October 2nd Granted special warrant against John Atkinson and John Cowper keelmen of Sunderland for assaulting Andrew and Benjamin Ph<*ar*>p shoemakers of ditto. [$2\frac{1}{2}$ *strokes; margin,* Agreed for the expenses; *inserted,* Nothing][43]

October 16th Made a mittimus for Richard Harrison vagrant for stealing a brood-goose of Mr Smithson's of Monk Wearmouth upon oath of John Henderson, John Bell and James Avery his servants, and bound them all over and Mr Smithson to prosecute under penalty of £10 each. *Note.* He was whipped privately.[44]

29th Granted general warrant against Alexander Wilson apprentice to John Wilson tobacconist of Gateshead for leaving his service. [*1 stroke*]

November 5th Granted general warrant against Edward Heaton butcher and Robert Tinmouth keelman, both of Monk Wearmouth for putting 6 half anchors of [*inserted,* foreign] brandy into the dwelling house and hogsty of Robert Thompson butcher (a vile rogue) upon his oath and wife's, that it was against his and her will, knowledge or desire. Dismissed the warrant.[45] [*1 stroke*]

Granted special warrant against Robert Potts farmer of Hebburn for detaining wages (8s) from Jane Dixon his hired servant. Note: the master paid 12s for wages and charges. [*1 stroke*]

9th Granted special warrant against Isable and Michael Hunter of Monk Wearmouth for cutting the cheek and abusing Mary Hutchinson of ditto. *Ordered Isable Hunter to pay 10s 6d and charges.* [$2\frac{1}{2}$ *strokes*]

---

43 Pharp or Faup occurs elsewhere – a Sunderland shoemaker, June 1st 1756.

44 Richard Harrison was whipped privately in gaol for the offence and then removed to his settlement of Battersea, 16 January 1754: DRO, Q/S/OB 11, p. 72. Entry crossed through in black pencil; two red pencil strokes in left margin.

45 Entry crossed through in black pencil; two red pencil strokes in left margin.

[*page*] 14 *1753*

Granted special warrant against G. Bennet mariner and Thomas Smith shoemaker of Monk Wearmouth to be witnesses in the cause of Edward Heaton and Robert Thompson. [*1 stroke*]

November 24th Granted special warrant against William Yellowly of Hedworth for turning of<f> his hired boy Thomas Hunter before expiration of his time. Agreed, on William Yellowly's paying all. [*1 stroke*]

November 26th Granted special warrant against George Forster and Peter Jones of the chapelry of Tanfield for beating and threatening Barnabas and William Calvert, and taking 8s from William Calvert. [$2\frac{1}{2}$ *strokes*]

December [*blank*] Granted general warrant against Isable Cowen of Sunderland spinster for conveying away goods seized by Peter Ovington the bayliff. *Note*: Nothing could be proved against her, but her character is bad enough.[46] [*circle*]

[*page*] 15 *1754*[47]

January 3rd Wrote to Joseph Jefferson of Harton master and mariner to make up a complaint with John Davison, upon account of his son's wages and boarding with him.

Granted special warrant against Reynold Robson and Mary his wife [*inserted*, innholder of Sunderland] for defrauding Christiana the wife of Daniel Brown shoemaker, viz. 7 hanks of yarn, linnen apron and handkercheif by way of truck for geneva.
Agreed to deliver up all, and to pay expences. N.B. They had no bad character.[48] [$2\frac{1}{2}$ *strokes*]

February 8th Granted special warrant against Richard Hylton joyner and John Brown cobleman both of the chapelry of Shields

---

46 Entry crossed through in black pencil; two red pencil strokes in left margin; 'character is bad enough' underlined in red pencil.

47 Tew now begins the year on 1 January.

48 Entry crossed through in black pencil; two red pencil strokes in left margin.

for whipping and bruising Mary Bolam wife of Alexander Bolam trimmer and Jane Hutchinson spinster (both of them society people)[49] of the said chapelry.
Acquitted.[50] [$2\frac{1}{2}$ *strokes*]

[*There are no entries for March 1754.*]

April 3rd Granted general warrant against John Lamb apprentice for the leaving his master's service [*blank*] Tewart of Monk Wearmouth.
Parted them upon the apprentice's father paying £5. [*1 stroke*]

6th Granted special warrant against Robert Young sailor upon John Cunningham's swearing he is in fear of his life from him. [$2\frac{1}{2}$ *strokes*]

Granted special warrant against Benjamin Wedderburn for refusing to come to work with his master George Holmes brickmaker of Shields after receiving 6d earnest in his father's presence and by his consent. Agreed, the boy returning to his service. [*1 stroke*]

Granted special warrant against James Purvis farmer of Whitburn for refusing to lead 700 tuns of stones according to agreement betwixt him and John Bell of Monk Wearmouth limeburner.[51] [*1 stroke*]

[*page*] 16 *1754*

April 15th Granted general warrant against John Philip for leaving the service of James Forrest [*inserted,* bad] cobleman of Shields before his time. Ordered James Forrest to pay charges and dismissed John Philip from his service. [*1 stroke*]

Granted general warrant against Thomas Headlam for leaving his master Jeremiah Wake linnen weaver, to whom he was bound apprentice. [*circle*]

---

49 Society of Friends, i.e. Quakers.
50 Two red and two black pencil strokes in left margin.
51 Two red pencil strokes in left margin, themselves crossed through in black pencil.

16th Ordered John Brown [*inserted,* bad] son of William Brown [*inserted,* worse] of East Boldon into the stocks for drunkenness.

June 17th 1754 Granted special warrant against James Todd of Hylton Bridge farmer for turning away Jane Carr from her servitude without just cause.
James Todd took her again. [*1 stroke*]

Granted general warrant against Elizabeth Widdowfield for leaving the service of Joseph Hayton of Sunderland slopman.
Dismissed the servant. [*1 stroke*]

18th Granted general warrant against William Clement for leaving the service of his master Dr. Andrew of Scotch House. [*circle; margin,* Not found]

Granted special warrant against John Roxby of Sunderland blacksmith for refusing to pay 9s 11$\frac{1}{2}$d for wages due to Elizabeth Sympson.
He payed the wages and charges. [*1 stroke*]

24th Granted special warrant against John Roxby aforesaid for refusing to pay 18s and 8d to John Miller his hired servant. [*1 stroke; margin,* He payed.]

27th Granted special warrant against Sarah Steed widow of Sunderland for declaring that Margaret Long<*ev*>ill sold a pair of boots which she knew to be stolen. Agreed.[52] [*1 stroke*]

July 1st Granted special warrant against Lionel or Lisle Hendry of Sunderland keelman for forcibly carrying away and detaining from her mother Margaret Stephenson an infant of 16 called also Margaret. [*circle*]

[*page*] 17 *1754*

July 1st Granted special warrant against Thomas Mills for

52 One red pencil stroke in left margin.

stealing and carrying away several loads of muck the property of John Bell of Monk Wearmouth farmer.[53]
[*deleted*, Mem. Warrant not paid for] [*1 stroke*]

9th Granted special warrant against William Pearson of Suddick[54] gardiner who, being drunk, came near the house of Jane Steel of the same place, and abused her and tore of<f> her [*inserted*, silk] handkercheif of<f> her neck to peices etc. [$2\frac{1}{2}$ *strokes; margin*, Agreed]

Granted special warrant against William Steedman and Isable his wife of the parish of Sunderland trimmer, for threatening the life of Ann the wife of George Telford cobleman of ditto, and for the said Isable throwing an hot poker against her. [$2\frac{1}{2}$ *strokes; margin*, Agreed]

Granted special warrant against John Roxby blacksmith of Sunderland for refusing to pay 12s wages to John North. [*1 stroke; margin*, He payed the money.]

22nd Granted general warrant against William Neessham of Sunderland shoemaker for a rape and giving the foul distemper to Sarah Turner an infant of 10 years of age. [*1 stroke; margin*, Committed to goal by Anthony Wilkinson Esq.][55]

24th Granted general warrant against George Johnson and Michael Cheriton for leaving the service of Thomas Dixon shipbuilder of Monk Wearmouth being his apprentices, and for being drunk and abusing the family. [*1 stroke; margin*, Agreed]

25th Granted special warrant against William Mason of Bishop Wearmouth carpenter and farmer for assaulting and striking

---

53 Entry crossed through in black pencil; one red pencil stroke in left margin.

54 I.e. Southwick.

55 William Neessham, or Neesham, of Sunderland, cobler, was acquitted at the assizes, 1754, PRO, DURH 16/1, DURH 17/7. The rape occurred in Sunderland workhouse. Anthony Wilkinson of Crossgate (City of Durham) was one of the most active justices on the bench in the 1750s, involved in key activities of the sessions; DRO, Q/S/OB 11, pp. 206–7 and *passim*. He first appeared on the commission of the peace in 1735, PRO, C192/2 part 2. Three red strokes in left margin, themselves crossed through in black pencil.

Thomas Bowhanan and breaking the head of Susanna his wife who is 6 months gone with child.
Note: William Mason agreed to pay 10s.[56] [2½ *strokes*]

[*page*] 18 *1754*

July 25th Granted special warrant against William Nicholson shoemaker of Monk Wearmouth for defrauding Esther wife of Henry Todd of ditto alehousekeeper of a note of £2 17s 6d drawn by Thomas Stoker shoemaker. [*1 stroke; margin,* Note] William Nicholson agreed to pay the money to Esther Todd.

26th Granted special warrant against William Todd junior of Monk Wearmouth for assaulting and giving a black eye to Richard Young apprentice of his father William Todd shipwright. [2½ *strokes; margin,* Agreed]

Granted special warrant against Mary Gallery of South Shields for stealing coals out of the yard of Thomas Fairles attorney at law. [*circle; margin,* Agreed]

Mem. Made up the affair of an attempt to ravish the daughter of George Mason of Whitburn gardiner by George Man junior, upon his paying her an year's wages and dismissing her.[57] [*circle*]

27th Granted special warrant against James Dunn of Westo labourer for assaulting and beating Thomas Layton a lame man of the same place and threatening his life. [2½ *strokes*]

31st Granted special warrant against John Bell of Monk Wearmouth farmer for dismissing his servant John Haslop before the due time without wages and beating him. [*1 stroke*]

---

56 Two red pencil strokes in left margin, themselves crossed through in black pencil.

57 Six red pencil strokes in left margin, themselves crossed through in black pencil.

August 6th Granted special warrant against John Craigs sailor for riding away with the horse of Matthew Thompson of Monk Wearmouth. [*1 stroke*]

[*deleted, Mem.*]

[page] 19 *1754*

September 4th
Granted special warrant against Lionel or Lyel Hendry, keelman of Sunderland and Margaret Stephenson spinster for beating bruising and threatening the life of her mother Margaret Stephenson. [$2\frac{1}{2}$ *strokes*]

Mem. September 26th On this day I convicted Richard Matthew limeburner of being drunk, upon my own view and sent out a warrant for the penalty 5s which he paid by George Sheville to the churchwarden.
N.B. I returned this conviction to the general quarter sessions on the 9th day of October 1754.[58]

October 23rd Granted special warrant against Thomas Bartrim servant to widow Taylor miller of Hebburn Fell for setting fire to the whins upon the said Fell and endangering the ricks and stacks of Thomas Marshall etc.[59] [$2\frac{1}{2}$ *strokes*]

November 2nd Granted special warrant against Thomasine Carter wife of Stephen Carter of Sunderland joiner for assaulting <and> beating Isable Taylor wife of Richard Taylor mariner, and drawing of<f> a gold ring from her finger, and throwing the said Isable's infant out of her arms etc. [$2\frac{1}{2}$ *strokes*]

13th Elizabeth Moore of South Shields single-woman swore the child or children of which she is now pregnant upon Abraham

---

58 Richard Matthew forfeited his recognizance of £20 because, when it was entered into on 26th September, he 'did insult and grossly abuse Edmund Tew, Doctor of Divinity' in the execution of his office; DRO, Q/S/OB 11, p. 111. Note that William Matthew, who is also listed on July 13–14th 1752, tanner, was involved in this incident.

59 Entry crossed through in black pencil; two red pencil strokes in left margin.

Brown her master, skipper and aleseller in South Shields, and that it was gotten on the 4th April last past.[60] [*1 stroke*]

29th Granted special warrant against Catherine the wife of William Swan for cruelly beating two of the children of Elinor Southern of Sunderland and threatening her.
Agreed. [2½ *strokes*]

[*page*] 20 *1754*

December 2nd Granted special warrant against William Finch of Sunderland [*inserted*, broken] butcher for beating and bruising Robert Cuthbertson and John Mountain carpenters of the same place and threatening to shoot Cuthbertson. [2½ *strokes*]

3rd William Finch [*inserted*, butcher] entered into recognizance for his good behaviour in the penal sum of £20 – Robert Thompson constable in £10 – both of Sunderland, Thomas French carpenter in £10 – Returned to the court.

4th Granted special warrant against James Farthing of South Shields wherryman for beating and bruising Archibald Bowey of the same place wherryman. [2½ *strokes; margin*, Agreed]

7th Granted special warrant against Thomas and Rebecca Wilkin of Sunderland grocer for turning away his hired servant Sarah Wright before the expiration of her term.
Agreed upon the mistress paying 7s 6d to the maid. [*1 stroke*]

Granted special warrant against Elisabeth Rawling wife of John of Monk Wearmouth ship carpenter for getting drunk and assaulting Mrs Elisabeth Chambers of the same place wife of Mr William Chambers.
Agreed. [*circle*]

13th Granted special warrant against Edward Weir of Shields

60 Entry crossed through in black pencil.

salter for breaking open the door of Jane Thompson and bruising her and daughter Ann etc.
Agreed. [2½ *strokes*]

Granted special warrant against Lawrence Lakeling of Shields labourer for knocking down and breaking the ribs of Janet Lesly wife of James Oswald of ditto labourer.
Debet. [2½ *strokes*]

Granted special warrant against George Wilson of Whitburn fisherman for refusing to deliver a tarpawlin, which he pretends to have found, the property of John Bell farmer.
Agreed upon Bell paying 2s 6d. [*1 stroke*]

[*page*] 21 *1754*

December 14th Information [*inserted,* was] made before me by Elizabeth Wright of Shields that Thomas and Isable Richardson [*inserted,* blacksmith] were both drunk on Thursday the 12 instant at Shields, upon which I sent out a summons warrant to them to appear.
Note: the woman did not stand to her oath.[61] [*1 stroke*]

18th Granted special warrant against Robert Gibson of Shields butcher for assaulting and beating Anne the wife of Robert Glover of Shields butcher, who is now very ill.
Agreed. [2½ *strokes*]

20th Granted special warrant against Mark Watson for not coming to the service of Mary Rochester of Shields widow having been hired by her and received earnest 5s.
Agreed upon payment of £1 to Mary Rochester. [*1 stroke*]

21st Granted special warrant against Mary Marshall, John Marshall and John Kilner for assaulting and threatening William Feaster, all of Bishop Wearmouth. [2½ *strokes; margin,* Agreed.]

---

61 Entry crossed through in black pencil; two red pencil strokes in left margin.

1755

February 10th Granted special warrant against John Bell of Southwick farmer for beating and bruising his hired servant John Heslop and kicking him out of his house and refusing to give him his cloaths or money.
Parted them and Bell paid all charges.[62] [$2\frac{1}{2}$ *strokes*]

22nd Granted special warrant against Robert Hincks and another pockbroken youth (whose name is not known) both of Sunderland for cutting down and carrying away the goods of William Kirk shopkeeper of Monk Wearmouth, and interrupting him for an year past in his business.[63] [$2\frac{1}{2}$ *strokes*]

[*page*] 22 *1755*

February 27th Granted special warrant against Elizabeth Fell hackney horse letter of Sunderland widow for locking in George Attis into her room, knocking him down and endeavouring to scald him with boyling water.[64] [$2\frac{1}{2}$ *strokes; margin,* Agreed]

March 3rd Granted special warrant against Thomas Pearson of Bishop Wearmouth barber for not learning his trade to his apprentice James Scriven and for beating and overloading him. [*circle*]

27th Granted special warrant against James Hardy glassman of Shields for detaining the wages of William Thompson being £1 2s 0d now due to his late wife Elizabeth Haydon. [*1 stroke*]

28th Granted special warrant against Robert Harper of Shields farmer for bruising Thomas Mills etc. [*circle*]

31st Granted special warrant against Peter Wanless of Southwick

---

62 Entry crossed through in black pencil; three red pencil stroks in left margin.

63 Entry crossed through in black pencil; two red pencil strokes in left margin; 'pockbroken' underlined in red pencil.

64 Entry crossed through in black pencil; five red and two blue pencil strokes in left margin; 'into' and 'knocking' underlined in red pencil.

farmer, for beating a lame man John Wood labourer of the same place for refusing his muck.[65] [2½ *strokes*]

Granted special warrant against George and Margaret Taylor the wife, pawnbroker of Sunderland and taylor, for buying the coat of Robert Dodd shipcarpenter of Monk Wearmouth knowing it to be stolen. [2½ *or 3 strokes; margin,* Agreed upon their returning the goods and paying charges.]

[*page*] 23 *1755*

5th April 1755 Granted special warrant against Elizabeth wife of George Murray alias Morriss of Sunderland comber, for throwing a brick and bruising etc. Magdalen Grainger wife of [*blank*] Grainger cooper [*inserted,* big with child] and threatening to cleave her down. [2½ *strokes*]

Granted special warrant against John Dent of Sunderland cobleman for beating Joseph Fleming taylor of the same, for only asking for his Majesty's land tax.[66] [2½ *strokes*]

Granted general warrant against Joseph Green apprentice to James Small of Sunderland chimney-sweeper for leaving his master's service before the expiration of his 7 years' term. [*1 stroke*]

April 14th Granted special warrant against Thomas Dixon of Monk Wearmouth mariner for beating and bruising Jane the wife of John Johnson taylor, all of Monk Wearmouth. [2½ *strokes*]

15th Granted special warrant against Thomas Cam alias Combe, sub-officer in the salt duties, for beating bruising and grossly abusing Rebecca Delaval wife of George Delaval mariner all of Shields, and t[e]aring her hat and gown etc. [2½ *strokes*]

16th Granted special warrant against Bartholomew Lumley, vitriol saltmaker, William Blagdon blacksmith, John Wilkinson

---

65 Entry crossed through in black pencil; two blue pencil strokes in left margin.

66 Entry crossed through in black pencil; two blue pencil strokes in left margin; 'his Majesty's' underlined in blue pencil.

barber, all of Shields, for giving two half gills of geneva with snuff to a natural fool Mary Browel, alias Cull Polly, by drinking which she has been at death's door and is still very ill and unable to work as usually, upon the information of her guardian Jane Dixon widow and saltmaker.[67] [$2\frac{1}{2}$ *strokes; margin,* Agreed upon their paying a guinea to Mary Browel.][68]

[*page*] 24 *1755*

April 18th Wrote a letter to Mr William Smitcham of Sunderland shopkeeper and agent to Mr Nicholson, to pay the arrears due for the maintenance of a bastard child begot by Mr Nicholson's son deceased on the body of Elinor Hugel.[69] [*circle*]

Granted special warrant against Ann Kewit spinster of Sunderland for detaining several goods left in pawn with her (being not licensed) by Bartholomew Dixon. [*2 strokes*]

May 6th Granted general warrant against Elinor R<*e*>y of Shields spinster for carrying away 3 pounds and 3 quarters salt which had not paid duty on the oaths of Thomas and John Cam salt officers.
Ordered the offender to pay 8s for the salt and expences.[70] [*1 stroke*]

10th Granted special warrant against William Maxwell labourer and Jane his wife for assaulting with an iron pot and <in> other ways abusing James Henderson labourer all of Bishop Wearmouth. [$2\frac{1}{2}$ *strokes*]

19th Granted special warrant against George Turner farmer of

---

67 Entry crossed through in black pencil; two blue pencil strokes in left margin.

68 A 'natural fool' or 'idiot' was defined in law quite strictly as one who had been *non compos mentis* from birth: Michael Dalton, *The Countrey Justice etc.* (London, 1666), p. 284. See P. Rushton, 'Idiocy, the Family and the Community in Early Modern North-East England', in D. Wright and A. Digby (eds), *From Idiocy to Mental Deficiency: Historical Perspectives on People with Learning Disabilities* (London, 1996), pp. 44–64.

69 Entry crossed through in black pencil.

70 Entry crossed through in black pencil; four blue strokes in left margin.

Jarro Slake for detaining £1 for wages due to Elinor Hoey. [*1 stroke; margin,* Ordered George Turner to pay the £1.]

Wrote to Mr John Sympson of Shields apothecary about turning away Joan Hutchinson. [*1 stroke; margin,* Mem Parted them.]

20th Granted special warrant against Alexander Southerland taylor of Sunderland for detaining 3s wages from John Gray. [*circle*]

Granted special warrant against William Parker servant of Sarah Yellowly of Southwick Hill House in Monk Wearmouth to swear to his knowledge concerning the hiring of her maid servant Mary Gustard. [*1 stroke*]

[*page*] 25 *1755*

Granted special warrant against William Ellimore and Lawrence Grey of Sunderland fishermen for feloniously taking and carrying away 4 oars the property of Ann Rush widow of the same. Ordered her half a guinea. [*circle*]

July 1st Granted special warrant against Jane the wife of George Tellfit an unlicensed pawnbroker of Sunderland for detaining 2 gowns, petticoat, sheets etc. of George Robson labourer of the same. [*1 stroke*]

15th Granted special warrant against Isable the wife of Thomas Turner alehousekeeper for assaulting William Watson constable of Sunderland in the execution of his office. [*circle*]

19th Granted general warrant against Thomas Jameson apprentice to George Lightfoot of Sunderland tallow chandler for leaving his master's service. [*1 stroke*]

22nd Granted special warrant against John Robson of Gateshead taylor for discharging his apprentice Thomas Reede without cause. [*1 stroke*]

Granted special warrant against Mary Sympson servant of Thomas Rippon of Bolden farmer for beating her dame etc. [*1 stroke*]

Committed [*inserted,* to Durham Gaol] Lucy Mills of Whitburn spinster for entring the house of Mary Shepherd of Whitburn, and stealing some meal, upon the oaths of the said Mary Shepherd, Thomasine Kirton and Thomas Purvis, whom I bound over to prosecute and give evidence, Mary Shepherd in £20, Thomasine Kirton and Thomas Purvis each in £10.[71]

[*page*] 26 *1755*

August 1st Granted special warrant against John Bell farmer of Monk Wearmouth for beating Thomas York his servant in a cruel manner.
Parted them, and Bell paid all charges.[72] [$2\frac{1}{2}$ *strokes*]

Wrote to Mr Surveyor of Sunderland to pay a poor man 10s 2d due for wages. [*circle*]

4th Granted special warrant against Adam Turner of Sunderland cabinet maker, Thomas Weems and others apprentices for beating and wounding Thomas Cust a fellow apprentice.
They paid the charges. [$2\frac{1}{2}$ *strokes*]

5th Granted special warrant against John Kirkup for beating and trampling upon the breast of Isable Pye of Shields aged 85, whereby her life is now in danger. Committed to House of Correction for want of sureties.[73] [$3\frac{1}{2}$ *strokes*]

6th Granted special warrant against John Brown of Westo blacksmith for not allowing sufficient victuals and cloaths to his apprentice John Islander.
Note The master discharged him rather than appear. [*circle*]

7th Granted special warrant against Charles Pattison ship-wright of Sunderland for beating and throwing under the hot bars of a fire, John Marshall apprentice.
Ordered the charges to be paid by Pattison.[74] [$2\frac{1}{2}$ *strokes*]

---

71 Mills was acquitted at the assizes in 1755; PRO, DURH 16/1.
72 See a similar complaint by a servant, September 29th 1756.
73 Entry crossed through in black pencil; three blue pencil strokes in left margin.
74 Entry crossed through in black pencil; three blue pencil strokes in left margin.

Granted special warrant against Joseph Taylor an under-surveyor of Sunderland for refusing to pay 10s 2d due to Ambrose Lennox, and for throwing him down stairs and thereby bruising him etc. Joseph Taylor paid 7s.[75] [*circle*]

[*page*] 27 *1755*

August 6th Margaret Skeen of Monk Wearmouth swore this day a bastard child against James Young of ditto mariner, about 3 weeks after Easter. [*1 stroke*]

7th Granted general warrant to Matthew Broderick one of the overseers of Monk Wearmouth to apprehend the above James Young. [*1 stroke*]

11th Granted special warrant against Jane wife of William Coward limeburner in Sunderland for beating Elinor wife of William Scot and abusing her good name and fame – *Note* Elinor Scot was proved a whore, and perjured, and paid the charges.[76] [$2\frac{1}{2}$ *strokes*]

14th Granted general warrant against Thomas Brown, John Dixon, and Robert Pattison for leaving the [*inserted*, service] of master Benjamin Finch of Sunderland ballast-keelman before the agreed for time.
They paid for the time and charges. [*1 stroke*]

15th Granted special warrant against John Chamberlain master and mariner for cruelly beating his apprentice. [*1 stroke*]

22nd Granted special warrant against George Mitchel of Yarmouth master and mariner for cruelly beating his apprentice Cuthbert Pringle.
Not found. [*1 stroke*]

---

75 One blue pencil stroke in left margin.

76 Entry crossed through in black pencil; three blue pencil strokes in left margin; 'proved a whore, and perjured' underlined in blue pencil.

Granted special warrant against Elizabeth wife of James Annesly of Shields shoemaker for wounding and laming Elizabeth daughter of Ann Fogo.
Ordered Annesly to pay surgeon and charges and to give 2s 6d. to the girl. [*2 strokes and circle*]

[*page*] 28 *1755*

August 22nd Granted special warrant against John Markham of Sunderland master and mariner for cruelly beating his apprentice John Morris. Not found. [*1 stroke*]

25th Granted general warrant against John Marchbanks labourer for leaving the work of John Hindmarsh farmer [*inserted*, and quarry man] of Southwick. [*1 stroke*]

Wrote to Mr Gilbert Moss innholder at the W<hite > Lyon Sunderland to deliver the cloaths of his servant James Burliston.
He delivered them. [*circle*]

27th Adjudged the complaint of John Hindmarsh against his servant John Marchbanks to be true, and committed the said Marchbanks to the House of Correction at Durham for 3 weeks. [2 *strokes*]

29th Granted special warrant against Margaret Roxby of Monk Wearmouth widow daughter-in-law of [*blank*] Wheatley deceased for refusing to pay 7s wages [*inserted*, to], and detaining the cloaths of, Elinor Crosby (a bad girl). [*circle; margin*, Note: She paid the wages and constable.]

Granted special warrant against Jonas and Elizabeth Pearson trimmer of Sunderland for beating and threatening revenge to Walter Hunter of Sunderland staymaker.
Charges paid by Jonas Pearson. [$2\frac{1}{2}$ *strokes*]

September 1st. Granted special warrant against Thomas Young and James Matson servants to George Middleyard and John Forrest of Shields fishermen for leaving their services.
They returned to their services. [*1 stroke*]

2nd Granted special warrant against Thomas Maiden of Shields shoemaker for assaulting and bruising Margaret Davison of ditto. Agreed. [2 *strokes*]

[*page*] 29 *1755*

September 5th Granted special warrant against William Ramsay of Hylton farmer for not allowing sufficient quantity of victuals to his servant William Watson. [*1 stroke; margin,* Agreed]

6th Granted special warrant against George Thompson of Sunderland fitter for detaining 10s wages of Elinor Walton, and her cloaths. [*margin, Note*:] He paid wages and charges. [*1 stroke*]

8th Granted special warrant against John Gillchrist of Shields skipper for knocking down George Forrest etc. [*margin,* Not paid.]

Granted a liberate from the House of Correction to John Kirkup. [*1 stroke*]

23rd Granted special warrant against Isable Robson [*inserted,* spinster of Shields] upon suspicion of stealing 2 silver tea spoons, 2 handkerchiefs, a snuff box and French needle case (the last of which was found upon the said Isable) the goods of George Delaval of Shields, mariner.
Note: The man (as I believe) compounded, for her paying for them. [$2\frac{1}{2}$ *strokes*]

2<4th> Granted special warrant against Henry Side and George Appleby coblemen of Sunderland for running away with the coble of John Stephenson of ditto.
[*margin,* Mem.] They paid 18s costs, and 3s 6d charges. [$2\frac{1}{2}$ *strokes*]

25th [*deleted,* Committed Isable Robson of Shields spinster to Durham gaol upon suspicion of the above felony. Recalled.]

[*page*] 30 *1755*

September 26th Granted general warrant against William Harrison apprentice for deserting the service of Mr William Jackson of Sunderland master and mariner. [*1 stroke*]

29th Granted special warrant against Edward Snowden and William Bell of Sunderland for breaking a lock and carrying away the skip boat of John Coulson master and mariner of Sunderland. Agreed upon paying 5s charges. [*1 stroke*]

Granted special warrant against Alexander Johnson for leaving the service of Benjamin Finch of Sunderland ballast man. [*One stroke*]

Granted general warrant against John Steward apprentice for leaving the service of John Moor shoemaker of Sunderland.

Granted special warrant against Joseph Jefferson of Monk Wearmouth master for cruelly using and threatening his apprentice Ralph Coltman. [*1 stroke*]

Granted special warrant against Oliver Jackson of Shields, master for taking away the good name and fame of John Gibson of ditto pilot.
Agreed.[77] [*circle*]

Passed Thomas Leighton with Mary his wife from Whitburn to Nether Witton chapelry Northumberland. [*3 strokes*]

[*page*] 31 *1755*

Granted special warrant against Charles Pinshion master and mariner for detaining 15s 7d from Ingram Johnson sailor of Sunderland. [*1 stroke*]

October 9th Granted general warrant against John Hardy of Monk Wearmouth for disobeying his master's lawfull demands and threatening to leave his service, viz., Thomas Dixon of Monk Wearmouth shipbuilder. [*1 stroke*]

13th Granted special warrant against Matthew Robinson of Shoreside alehousekeeper and keelman for assaulting, beating and threatening John Bridon of the same labourer. [$2\frac{1}{2}$ *strokes*]

---

77 Entry crossed through in black pencil; two blue pencil strokes in left margin; 'taking away the good name and fame of' underlined in blue pencil.

15th Committed to Durham gaol John Bridon of Monk Wearmouth labourer for saying before the constable of ditto, Matthew Robinson and another, 'That he could not and had not justice' done to him the said Bridon; in relation to a dispute between him and the said Robinson, wherein I awarded Matthew Robinson to pay all expenses for warrant and constable and 2s for the day's work lost by John Bridon.
Mem On the 16th I released him at Durham upon falling on his knees and paying 10 shillings to the constable for horse hire etc.[78]

[*page*] 32 *1755*

Granted general warrant against Richard Cropton of Robin Hoods Bay, [*inserted*, and now riding in the port of Sunderland] master and mariner for detaining the wages of John Seymour £7 14s 0d, John Easton £7 17s 8d, and Daniel Taylor £6 13s 2d. [3 *strokes*]

October 21st Granted general warrant against Anthony Hale and George Hoy of Swalwell keelmen for wantonly assaulting and bruising the head and back of William Campbell gardiner at Hebburn Hall. Agreed. [*circle*]

November 6th Thomasine Shipley of Jarro singlewoman swore the child she is now pregnant with to Joseph White, churchwarden of Chester. [*1 stroke*]

7th Granted special warrant against Joseph White of Chester-le-Street church-warden for getting the said Thomasine with child upon complaint of John Jefferson overseer of Jarro. [*1 stroke*]

10th Granted special warrant against Jane the wife of [*blank*] Maxfield and John Douglass keelman both of Bishop Wearmouth for

78 Entry crossed through in black pencil; two blue pencil lines in left margin; 'could not and had not justice'' done', 'awarded' and 'his knees' underlined in blue pencil.

bruising the eye and threatening the life of Thomas Brown of ditto keelman on the 6th instant. [$2\frac{1}{2}$ *strokes*]

[There are no entries for December 1755 – April 1756.]

[*page*] 33 *1756*

Granted special warrant against Laurence Lakeling, Charles Wilson and Harry called the miller, all glassmen of South Shields for riotously entring the house of Sarah Precise drunk during time of divine service and breaking up the rails leading thereto. Agreed. [$2\frac{1}{2}$ *strokes*]

May 4th Granted general warrant against Robert Ridley of Gateshead for deserting the service of Alexander Galls of Monk Wearmouth master and mariner. [*1 stroke*]

Granted special warrant against [*blank*] of Shields for calling a woman whore and theif and being a common brawler.
Acquitted. [$2\frac{1}{2}$ *strokes*]

Granted general warrant to Mr Jeremiah Abbs of Monk Wearmouth against his apprentice for leaving his service. [*circle*]

10th Granted special warrant against William Forster servant of Robert Thompson of Bishop Wearmouth upon the information of Ann Humble servant to William Smith of Boldon, that she was with child by him.
Note John Forster of East Boldon farmer and Robert Forster of Southwick labourer entered into recognizance of £20 each, for his appearing at the next quarter sessions.
Mem. He marryed her.[79] [$3\frac{1}{2}$ *strokes*]

Granted special warrant against John Dobson of Barnston [*inserted,* in Washington parish] (who marryed John Heath's sister) for detaining the wages of William Trotter. Agreed. [*1 stroke*]

---

79 William Forster was reported at the quarter sessions, DRO, Q/S/OB 11, p.249. One blue pencil stroke in left margin; 'she was' underlined in blue pencil.

14th Granted special warrant against Patrick Bryce and Robert Thompson (the apprentices of two butchers of Sunderland) for breaking windows, lock of the house, and beating and abusing Isable Waller wife of Michael Waller of Sunderland labourer whose house they entred, and cut 12 dozen of wheel bands and carryed or cast away the iron hoops of a tub etc. [$2\frac{1}{2}$ *strokes*]

[*page*] 34 *1756*

May 19th Granted general warrant against Jane Henderson for leaving the service of Mr Jer<emiah> Abbs of Monk Wearmouth.[80] [*1 stroke*]

24th Dorothy Richardson of Harraton spinster swore her self with child by George Davison of ditto waggonman. [*circle*]

Granted general warrant against the said George Davison upon application from the overseer [*inserted*, George Fisher] and gave the fees to John Huntley of Gateshead. [*circle*]

Granted general warrant against Deborah Forster widow of the parish of Jarro for detaining £2 15s 0d the wages of Jane Leech her servant.
Note: She paid all. [*1 stroke*]

May 31st Elinor Hutchinson [*inserted*, alias Hodgson] of Aberdeen spinster swore that she was now with child by John Gibson taylor of Hedworth from the 9th January last and the said John Gibson took his oath before me that he would marry her as soon as they could be asked in the churches of Jarro and Bishop Wearmouth.
Note: He afterwards ran away.[81] [*circle*]

Granted general warrant against Ralph Curry besom-maker of Chester-le-Street upon complaint of John Walker for robbing the rookery, spoiling the garden beds and trees in the deanery garden there, hired now by John Walker.[82] [*circle*]

---

80 'Mr Jer. Abbs' underlined in blue pencil.
81 Entry crossed through in black pencil; two blue pencil strokes in left margin; 'He afterwards' underlined in blue pencil.
82 Entry crossed through in black pencil.

[*page*] 35 *1756*

June 1st Granted special warrant against Robert Thompson and Benjamin Faup both shoemakers of Sunderland for beating etc. another shoemaker of ditto. Agreed. [2½ *strokes*]

7th Martha Clark of Shields singlewoman swore that the child she is now pregnant with, is by James Miller of Shields, glassman and alehousekeeper. [*1 stroke*]

9th Granted general warrant against William Greenwell of the Shoreside alehousekeeper and William Turner his partner in quarrys for detaining £2 5s 10d from Jesse Graydon miller for work. [*1 stroke*]

11th Granted special warrant against William Donnison of Monk Wearmouth keelman for wounding and bruising Simon Longstaff of the same ditto.
Agreed. [2½ *strokes*]

12th Granted general warrant against William Thirtle for leaving the service of Patrick Campbell, owner of the Sea Nymph. [*1 stroke*]

August 10th Elizabeth Orton of Haughton near Darlington spinster swore her male bastard child of whom she was delivered on the 21st June last to Mr William Moore druggist of the same place. [*1 stroke*]

12th Write to Henry Hays master of the Moidore to return the cloaths of Edward Parkinson sailor. [*1 stroke*]

16<th> Granted general warrant against John Thwaits of Sunderland skipper for 3s 9d wages due to William Maude. [*1 stroke*]

[*page*] 36 *1756*

August 26th 1756 Granted general warrant against George Urens, alias Orange, for leaving the work of his master [*blank*] Maxfield brickmaker of Shields. [*1 stroke*]

26th Granted general warrant against Roger Eden of Bishop Wearmouth trimmer and Elizabeth his wife for striking and threatening with a knife Margaret the wife of Thomas Watson of the same parish keelman. [$2\frac{1}{2}$ *strokes*]

30<th> Granted special warrant against John Cameron wherry-boat-man from Sunderland to the Shoreside for wounding William Greaves mariner of K<ings> Lynn in Norfolk with an iron boat hook in his left arm. [*1 stroke*]

31st Granted special warrant against Mary Hannah and Isable Porteous of Bishop Wearmouth for keeping a disorderly house upon the oaths of [*blank*].
Note The overseers agreed with them to drop the prosecution. [$2\frac{1}{2}$ *strokes*]

Granted general warrant against Ann Rowel for leaving the service of Edward and Ann Young of Shields, saltmaker. [*1 stroke*]

September 4th *Mem*. Gerrard Atmar, mariner, and Robert Walker of Sunderland alehousekeeper entered into recognizance to answer the complaint of the above William Greaves mariner against John Cameron wherry-boat-man. The former in £100, the latter in £50 to see John Cameron forthcoming at the next general quarter sessions at Durham.[83] [*2 strokes and a figure* 4]

[*page*] 37 *1756*

September 4th Granted general warrant against Ralph Clarke of Monkton farmer for wages £1 17s 9d due to John Lindsly. I agreed the matter betwixt them. [*1 stroke*]

Granted special warrant against Thomas Jefferson of Shields keelman for beating and bruising his mother-in-law Isable Young of ditto widow.
Not paid.

---

83 Atmar or Attmore was fined 6d at the quarter sessions: DRO, Q/S/OB 11, p. 247.

Made a mittimus to the House of Correction at Durham for Elizabeth Jefferson for refusing to return to her work.
Agreed and superseded it. [*1 stroke*]

10th Granted special warrant against [*blank*] Layton exciseman of Shields for breaking open the door of Mary Younghusband of ditto, and threatening her with some bodily harm and throwing stones against the house for an hour.
Agreed. [$2\frac{1}{2}$ *strokes*]

14th Granted special warrant against Ann wife of James Coltman of Sunderland mariner for pulling down stairs, and thereby greatly bruising Frances Coltman of Sunderland manteau-maker. [$2\frac{1}{2}$ *strokes*]

16th Granted special warrant against Edward Young [*inserted,* saltmaker of Shields] for assaulting, throwing upon the bed, with an intent to lye with Dorothy the wife of William Jefferson keelman of Shields. [$2\frac{1}{2}$ *strokes*]

25<th> Granted special warrant against Alice Morton of Shields widow for calling Catherine Holliday shopkeeper of the same whore and thief etc.
Note Catherine Holliday is a contentious person, as is her brother. [$2\frac{1}{2}$ *strokes*]

[*page*] 38 *1756*

September 23rd Granted special warrant against Bartholomew Lumley of Shields chymist for breaking windows, and beating Mary Kirkup and threatening the life of Millicent Scot.
Agreed upon Lumley's submission, never more to disturb her and his paying 8s 6d. [$2\frac{1}{2}$ *strokes*]

26th Granted general warrant against George Wilkinson late of Birtley farmer for threatening the lives of his father John and brother and sister of Westo. [$2\frac{1}{2}$ *strokes*]

27th Granted special [*inserted,* summons] warrant against William Huitson of Jarro ballast-heaver for charging James Henderson of the same blacksmith with stealing chickens. [*1 stroke*]

Granted special warrant against Margaret wife of John Sparks of Sunderland shoemaker for assaulting and bruising Margaret the wife of John Thornton of the same keelman. [$2\frac{1}{2}$ *strokes*]

29th Granted special warrant against John Hall alehousekeeper of Sunderland for bruising and violently throwing against a door Dinah Smirwit his servant.
Agreed for him to pay the charges. [$2\frac{1}{2}$ *strokes*]

Granted special warrant against John Bell farmer of Monk Wearmouth for turning away his servant George Shanks and detaining the wages of his wife 7s 9d. [*1 stroke*]

30th Granted special warrant against William Coxon of the Shoreside mariner for assaulting and t<e>aring the gown [*inserted,* sleeve] of Elisabeth wife of [*blank*] Wallis cordwainer and threatening her. [*inserted,* Dismissed the warrant and N.B. Elizabeth Wallis is a bad woman] [$2\frac{1}{2}$ *strokes*]

[*page*] 39 *1756*

September 30th Granted special warrant against Robert Harrison of Shields cobleman for charging a theft of 8s or 10s upon James Boteler and two others of Shields. [$2\frac{1}{2}$ *strokes; margin,* Ordered Robert Harrison to pay 6<s> 6d expenses.]

October 1st Wrote to Robert Wallis boatbuilder of Shields to pay 5 weeks' wages due to Sarah Lawley. [*circle*]

4th Gave an order to the overseers of the poor for Sunderland to provide for Sarah daughter of Elinor Stead, a bastard, till they can pass her to Blackburn in Lancashire the place of her settlement. [*1 stroke*]

11th Granted special warrant against William Matson for beating John Hutchinson, both of Shields coblemen.
Agreed. [*3 or possibly* $2\frac{1}{2}$ *strokes*]

Granted special warrant against Mary wife of [*blank*] for bruising Samuel Reeves of Bishop Wearmouth.
Agreed. [$2\frac{1}{2}$ *strokes*]

12th Granted special warrant against Emanuel Campbell of Shields pilot for assaulting and t<e>aring the coat of William Grainger of ditto innholder and calling him rogue and pirate. Agreed. [$2\frac{1}{2}$ *strokes*]

13th Granted special warrant against Elisabeth Coats wife of William Coats cobleman for abusing the good name and fame of Margaret wife of James Coxon cobleman.
Agreed.[84] [2 *strokes*]

[*page*] 40 *1756*

October 14th Granted special warrant against [*deleted,* Elisabeth Coates; *inserted,* Thomas Atkinson] of Sunderland master and mariner for abusing and beating John Briggs his apprentice. Dismissed, but *Note* Thomas Atkinson is a drunken [*inserted,* fellow] and when so a mad fellow. [*1 stroke*]

15th Granted special warrant against Ann wife of Cuthbert Hutchinson cobleman of Whitburn for defrauding James Ray and Edward Watson of salvage money.
Dismissed the said warrant. [*1 stroke*]

19th Granted special warrant against Thomas Punshion of Sunderland master of the ship Nancy for misusing William Swan his apprentice. [*1 stroke*]

24th Granted special warrant against Philip Frankland of Whitby in the County of York master and mariner upon suspicion of a rape on Jane Purvis [*inserted,* daughter of John and [*blank*] Purvis] of Shields an infant of 11 years old, and also against Elisabeth Barnet for aiding the said Philip Frankland.
Agreed. [$2\frac{1}{2}$ *strokes*][85]

---

84 'Name and fame' underlined in blue pencil.
85 One blue pencil stroke in left margin.

25th Granted special warrant against Mary Haddock [*inserted*, of Shields] for defrauding Ann and [*blank*] Brown of 1s 6d, belonging also to Shields.
Paid by Mary Haddock. [*1 stroke*]

28th Granted special warrant against Robert Carnaby of Shields butcher for trampling upon James Gibson of Shields butcher and threatening to throw him into the river. [$2\frac{1}{2}$ *strokes*]

30th Granted a pass to Jonathan Cumm an old discharged soldier from Lieutenant Colonel James Adolphus Oughton's Regiment of Foot for 21 days from this day, to Parkgate, the place of his settlement in Cheshire.[86] [*circle*]

[*page*] 41 *1756*

Granted special warrant against Hugh Ryout mariner and Sarah his wife of Monk Wearmouth for beating and bruising Dorothy wife of John Anderson innholder, breaking open 2 doors and threatening their lives, and Elizabeth Appleby spinster.
Released 3s 4d. [$2\frac{1}{2}$ *strokes*]

November 10th Granted general warrant against John Thompson and George Davison apprentices for leaving the service of Edward Browel late master and mariner, and now in<n>holder of Sunderland. [*1 stroke*]

Granted general warrant against John Gibson late of Hedworth taylor, at the request of William Cockburn of Sunderland overseer, in order to indemnifye the said parish against Elinor Hutchinson and her female infant born in the said parish on the 9th of October last. [*2 strokes*]

15th Granted special warrant against Robert Johnson of Shields master and mariner for defrauding George Tindal fisherman of a cock-chicken. [*deleted*, Not paid] Paid honestly.[87]

---

86 Two blue pencil strokes in left margin.

87 Two blue pencil strokes in left margin; 'Not paid' and 'Paid honestly' underlined in blue pencil.

18th Granted special warrant against John Bell of Monk Wearmouth farmer for defrauding Christopher Steel of Southwick blacksmith, by paying him a counterfeit half guinea. [*1 stroke*]

Granted special warrant against Elizabeth Pye of Shields widow and innholder for defrauding Jacob Forster tyleman by giving him an 18s peice for a guinea. [*1 stroke*]

[*page*] 42 *1756*

November 23rd Took the deposition of John Hall, alias Harle, [*inserted*, of Whitburn] in relation to Christopher Steel offering an half guinea in payment at Newcastle. [*1 stroke*]

23rd Committed John Bell to the county goal upon the deposition upon oath of William Richardson constable of Monk Wearmouth for calling me *fool* etc. and afterwards insulting me and threatening me with the King's Bench and that it was at my peril etc. not to take the oath of the above John Hall or Harle.
Superseded.[88]

Mem On the next day Mr Harrison fitter and Mr George Longstaff came to interceed for him, and upon his asking pardon upon his knees before all my parish and the constable, I forgave him upon paying one guinea to the poor of the parish of Boldon, 1 to Whitburn, and 1 to Monk Wearmouth, and all charges to constable etc.[89]

30th Granted general warrant against James Moore of Shields skipper for detaining 6s wages from George Nicholson of ditto keelman.
Not paid.

December 9th Granted warrant upon oath of William Potter of North Shields to persue, seize and keep for £3 arrears of rent the goods of Thomas Carr mariner of South Shields removed in the

88 Entry crossed through in black pencil; two blue pencil strokes in left margin.
89 Entry crossed through in black pencil; two blue pencil strokes in left margin; two short blue strokes in right margin beside 'his knees'.

night by his wife Elisabeth Carr from the tenement of the said William Potter. Agreed, nevertheless.
Mem. This warrant should have been signed by two Justices. [*1 stroke*]

[*page*] 43 *1756*

December 13th Granted general warrant against George Ranson apprentice to Frances Howes of Monk Wearmouth skipper, for leaving his said master's service. [*1 stroke*]

Granted special warrant against Edward Weir, alias Wears, of Shields, salter, for beating bruising and burning Henry Graham and Hannah his wife and Isable Rushwit.
Mem. All drunkards. *Note* Edward Weir paid the charges and 5s more to the sufferers. [$2\frac{1}{2}$ *strokes*]

27th Granted general warrant against Simon Miller of Shields taylor for detaining 7s 6d wages from John Langley. [*1 stroke*]

Granted special warrant against Thomas Donkin of Sunderland keelman for beating his wife Isable and turning her out of doors, and refusing her a maintenance, being unable to work by reason of her weakness. [*1 stroke*]

30<th> Granted special warrant against James Weatherburn, John Lakeling, glassmen, and Thomas Atty mariner all of Shields, for hiring the boat of Thomas Armstrong for Cullercoats and leaving her at Blythe. [*1 stroke*]

[*page*] 44 *1757*

January 8th Granted special warrant against John Atkinson of Shields innholder for assaulting, bruising Jane Kell and Sarah Olivers spinsters, t<e>aring their capuchins, caps and throwing them against the stones etc. Agreed at 10s 6d to the sufferers. [$2\frac{1}{2}$ *strokes*]

10th Granted special warrant against Jane Smith upon the complaint of the overseer of Monk Wearmouth to be examined touching her settlement. [*1 stroke*]

Granted special warrant against Elizabeth Harrison wife of James cobleman for assaulting Deborah Anderson of Shields, spinster, and beating her. [*1½ strokes*]

Granted special warrant against Ann Selby of Shields cakeseller for detaining the cloaths of Ann Young, spinster. [*1 stroke*]

11th Removed Jane Smith from Monk Wearmouth to the parish of Whickham upon her oath that she was born there and [*inserted,* had] acquired no other settlement. [*4 strokes*]

14th Granted general warrant to surveyor of the highways (William Harrison) of Southwick against several defaulters. [*1 stroke*]

15th Granted general warrant against William Graham of Harton weaver for detaining 14s and 1d from John Railtown Piercy. Agreed to take 10s within half an year and received of it 2s. [*circle*]

[*page*] 45 *1757*

January 24th Granted special warrant against Hugh Cow, alias Cough, of Shields, saltmaker, for assaulting and wounding James Reed keelman of the same. [*1½ strokes*]

Took the deposition of Ann Stoddard wife of William of Monk Wearmouth that she never directly or indirectly made information against any brandys found in the stack garth of William Booth at Hylton Boat. [*circle*]

February 19th Granted general warrant against William Bell brewer of Swalwell for beating bruising and threatening the life of John Wilson refiner of iron at Swalwell. [*2½ strokes*]

[*inserted,* Mem. Mr Burdon went to live at Hardwick.][90]

[There are no entries for March and April 1757.]

---

90 John Burdon moved to Hardwick Hall near Sedgefield, where he had grandiose plans for the house and gardens; G. B. Hodgson, *The Borough of South Shields from the Earliest Times to the Close of the Nineteenth Century* (Newcastle, 1903), p. 122; N. Pevsner, *The Buildings of England: County Durham*, 2nd edition revised by E. Wilkinson (Harmondsworth, 1983), p. 300.

May 23rd Granted special warrant against Ralph Welch the younger [*margin*, farmer] of Great Lumley batchelor, to give in security to the parish of Monk Wearmouth to maintain the child of Isable Hedley which she has this day sworn to him from about the 19th January last. [3 *strokes*]

Granted special warrant against James Dicks of Monk Wearmouth ship carpenter, for beating John Matthews, labourer to William Greenwell, of ditto and threatening his life. [2½ *strokes*]

26th Granted special warrant against John Young of Sunderland shipbuilder for assaulting, beating and threatening Robert Mills of the same labourer. [2½ *strokes*]

Four affidavits. [4 *strokes*]

[*page*] 46 *1757*

May 30th Granted general warrant against John Paul apprentice to [*blank*] Benson of Whitby for leaving his ship. [1 *stroke*]

Granted general warrant against George Macklean of Pallion for leaving the work of George Stoddard of Southwick quarryman. [*circle*]

Wrote to Jane Osborn of Shields shopkeeper for beating Jane Ponton, and breaking her door. [*circle*]

31st Granted special warrant against John Atkinson of Shields joiner for turning away Sarah Hudspeth his hired servant before the time.
Agreed for a quarter's wages to her. [1 *stroke*]

June 1st Granted special warrant against Ephraim Spraggons for refusing to go to the work of Mr John Thompson of Shields which he was hired to. He complyed. [1 *stroke*]

2nd Granted general warrant against William Wallace of Sunderland master and mariner for detaining £1 13s 4d wages due to Alexander Baker ship carpenter of Monk Wearmouth.
Agreed. [1 *stroke*]

Granted general warrant against George Young of Monk Wearmouth mariner for detaining 3s 6d wages due to Mary Rumford of ditto.
Note: he paid [*1 stroke*]

Granted special warrant against Henry Coats of Shields cobleman for beating Richard Reay cobleman of ditto.
Agreed that said Henry Coats should pay the charges, as he struck first, but *Note,* Richard Reay is a quarrelsome foulmouthed fellow. [*2 strokes*]

[*page*] 47 *1757*

June 5th Passed Martha Turner widow and Mary her daughter from Southwick to Long Haughton[91] in Northumberland. [$2\frac{1}{2}$ *strokes*]

Two affidavits from Mr Usher and John Humble his sea servant for 3 years [*2 strokes*]
Two more for another servant. [*2 strokes*]

12<th> Granted special warrant against John Anderson of Monk Wearmouth innholder for biting the arms of Catherine Appleby and Elizabeth her daughter and threatening the life of the said Elizabeth Appleby.
Note They are all whores and rogues. [$2\frac{1}{2}$ *strokes*]

14th Committed the above John Anderson to the goal at Durham, till he find sufficient sureties. [*circle*]
[*inserted,* Released on the 17th upon finding securities for good behaviour, and bound him over and gave my fee to Mr Man as formerly.] [*circle*]

15th Granted special warrant against Robert Bingham of Sunderland master and mariner for refusing to maintain his apprentice Thomas Masslett who has broke his leg, and to pay £2 15s 0d due to him for wages.
Mem. Robert Bingham paid charges, wages and for his apprentice's board. [*circle*]

91 I.e. Long Houghton.

18th Ordered the overseers of Washington to pay 2s per week to widow Snowden and 2 children and 1s per week to Jane Carr widow. [*circle*]

Granted special warrant against Thomas Gibson of Shields pilot for carrying away part of the wreck of a ship. [*1 stroke*]

20th Ordered the overseers of Bishop Wearmouth to take into their workhouse Jane Davison widow and her 3 children, and to pay the arrears due to her and them. [*circle*]

Granted special warrant against William Gibson butcher of Shields for turning away his servant Mary Marley without reason. [*1 stroke*]

[*page*] 48 *1757*

June 24th Granted special warrant against Dorothy the wife of James Rogerson for beating and knocking down and bruising Rebecca Delaval. [*2 strokes*]

Granted special warrant against Henry Deane skipper and Jane Fryar of Monk Wearmouth for taking away the good name and fame of Mary wife of John Magham of ditto mariner.
Agreed upon their paying charges. *Note* Mary Magham is a common woman.[92] [*1 stroke*]

25<th> Granted special warrant against James Ellison for taking away the good name and fame of John Innes of Aires[93] Key Bishop Wearmouth.[94]

Granted special warrant against Dorothy Cow or Cough wife of Hugh Cow saltmaker for taking away the good name of Sarah Reed of ditto.
Agreed, if they pay the charges.[95] [*1 stroke*]

---

92 Entry crossed through in black pencil; two blue pencil strokes in left margin.
93 I.e. Ayres.
94 Entry crossed through in black pencil; three blue pencil strokes in left margin.
95 Entry crossed through in black pencil; three blue pencil strokes in left margin.

Granted special warrant against Thomas Davison master [*inserted*, and mariner of Sunderland] for not maintaining his apprentice, and refusing to pay his wages.
N.B. He paid for all. [*circle*]

Granted special warrant against George Malbon keelman for cutting the bag of Richard Holiday of Bishop Wearmouth and threatening his life.
Not paid, and Richard sold the warrant and is a first villain. [*circle*]

Ruth Dixon singlewoman of Shields made oath that she was with child, and that George Snaith of Shields blacksmith is the father of it, from about Christmas. [*circle*]

[*margin*, Monday] 27th Granted special warrant against Elinor Bolt wife of Joseph Bolt of Bell Key[96] in Jarro waterman, for assaulting etc. Richard Nesbit glassmaker and Ann his wife. [2½ *strokes*]

[*page*] 49 *1757*

June 27th Monday Granted special warrant against Ralph Ellison of Shields shoemaker for assaulting etc. Elizabeth Hayton of ditto breadseller and breaking her sealed wooden measure etc. [2½ *strokes*]

29th Two affidavits from Harry Forster of Monk Wearmouth and his carpenter Longstaff. [*circle*]

July 1st Granted special warrant against Isable Clark of East Boldon widow for assaulting etc. Henry Pickering of ditto gentleman. [*circle*]

Bound over the said Isable Clark in £20, and Robert Matthew and Richard Walters yeomen in £10 each for her appearance at the next quarter sessions at Durham. Released. [3 *strokes*]

---

96 I.e. Bill Quay.

2nd Granted special warrant against Margaret Roxby of Monk Wearmouth [*inserted*, widow] for beating and bruising Sarah wife of Hugh Ryot mariner of ditto.
Note. They are both common strumpets. [*3 strokes*]

11th Granted general warrant against George Snaith of Shields blacksmith upon the oath of Ruth Dixon of ditto for getting her with child.
Note: he marryed her.[97] [$2\frac{1}{2}$ *strokes*]

Granted special warrant against Roger Eden trimmer of Bishop Wearmouth and Ann Eden his daughter for bruising and biting the breasts of Elizabeth wife of William Broderick of ditto.
Agreed upon paying charges.[98] [$2\frac{1}{2}$ *strokes*]

Granted special warrant against Roger Eden aforesaid for beating and threatening to stab Barbara Scot of Bishop Wearmouth spinster.
Agreed upon ditto. [$2\frac{1}{2}$ *strokes*]

13th Granted summons warrant against Alice Hodgson and Joseph Harper of Shields farmer for defaming Ann wife of his brother Robert Harper of ditto farmer. [*1 stroke*]

[*page*] 50 *1757*

July 15th Granted special warrant against William Maddison of Sunderland ship carpenter for beating and threatening Thomas Walker of ditto ship-carpenter. [$2\frac{1}{2}$ *strokes; margin*, Agreed]

18th Granted special warrant against Elinor Bigg and Margery Dixon servants of Mary Gofton of Shields saltmaker for refusing to go to work. [*1 stroke; margin*, Agreed]

Wrote to Mr Cock of Shields owner of the ship [*blank*] in behalf of his apprentice Lyddel's wages 18s. [*circle*]

---

97 Entry crossed through in black pencil; two blue pencil strokes in left margin.
98 Entry crossed through in black pencil; two blue pencil strokes in left margin.

20th Granted special warrant against Jane wife of James Young mariner of Sunderland for beating and threatening Margaret Rowntree wife of John of ditto mariner. [$2\frac{1}{2}$ *strokes; margin,* Agreed]

23rd Granted special warrant against Mary Howes [*inserted,* wife of Francis] of Monk Wearmouth innholder upon complaint upon oath of William Brymar of Sunderland watchseller that he laid down a silver watch in her house and lost it.
N.B. Brymar was drunk and was at several other houses so he paid all charges of horse hire etc. to Francis Howes being 5s.[99]
[*circle*]

26th Granted special warrant against Thomas Denton of Monk Wearmouth mariner and William Robinson of Sunderland mariner for beating and threatening to drown Thomas Heron servant of the ferryboat. [$2\frac{1}{2}$ *strokes; margin,* Agreed]

27th Granted general warrant against John Carr of Felton in Northumberland for leaving the service of Thomas Forster master and mariner of Monk Wearmouth to whom he is apprentice. [*circle; margin,* Not found]

[*page*] 51 *1757*

August 8th Granted special warrant against Isable Hall of Shields widow for defaming Jane Bond, calling her whore and thief and declaring she would prove her both.
Agreed upon her paying charges.[100] [$2\frac{1}{2}$ *strokes*]

10<th> Granted special warrant against William and J. Dods of Monk Wearmouth keelmen for beating Edward Watson ferryboatman.
Agreed. [$2\frac{1}{2}$ *strokes*]

Granted general warrant against Thomas Kensey mariner of Newcastle, upon the oath of Ann Richardson of Shields, that she

99 Entry crossed through in black pencil; two blue pencil strokes in left margin.
100 Entry crossed through in black pencil; three blue lines in left margin.

is with child by him, having this day taken her oath of the same. [2 *strokes*]

15<th> Wrote to the overseer of the poor [*inserted,* of Bishop Wearmouth] to give Elizabeth Revel and her 4 children 2s per week, or show cause etc. [*circle*]

Wrote to Barnston constablery to allow widow Taylor and 5 small children 2s 6d per week, or show cause etc. [*circle*]

17th I committed to goal Joseph Henderby of Sunderland labourer (being charged upon oath of Sarah Cornforth of ditto singlewoman before George Baker Esq. for getting her with child) for want of sureties.[101] [*circle*]

18<th> Granted special warrant against William Archer of Sunderland master and mariner for cruelly using his apprentice Thomas Hill, threatening his life, and refusing [*inserted,* to pay] his wages.
Agreed. [2½ *strokes*]

24th Granted special warrant against Elisabeth wife of Francis Watson mariner of the Shoreside for threatening the life and a mischeif to Stephen Buck of ditto taylor. [2½ *strokes; margin,* Agreed]

[*page*] 52 *1757*

August 26th Granted general warrant against 3 pitmen for deserting the work of Nicholas Lambton Esq.[102] [*circle; margin,* Agreed]

---

101 George Baker, son of a man of the same name from Crook, settled at Elemore Hall near Pittington. He was a well educated and assiduous magistrate, and largely responsible for the appearance of the house today: J. Venn and J.A. Venn (eds), *Alumni Cantabrigienses,* Part 1, vol. 1 (Nendeln, Liechtenstein, 1974), p. 70; Pevsner, *County Durham,* pp. 264–5.

102 Nicholas Lambton of South Biddick, Washington, was in active collaboration with John Burdon and John Baker (both justices referred to in Tew's Notebook) in various dealings: DRO, D/Br/D, 109 and 2635.

Took 2 Affidavits of Thomas Carr master and Thomas Carr apprentice of Panshia.[103] [2 *strokes*]

Granted general warrant against Thomas Chilton of Sunderland master and mariner for detaining £4 10s 0d from [*inserted,* Thomas] the son of Thomas Atkinson of Cleadon wheelwright. [*circle*]

27th Granted special warrant against Joseph Atkinson of Monk Wearmouth master and mariner for assaulting David Marshall of Sunderland boatman, taking away his boathook and threatening to stab him etc. [$2\frac{1}{2}$ *strokes; margin,* Agreed]

29th Granted general warrant against John Clark apprentice to William Nicholson of Monk Wearmouth shoemaker for leaving the service of his master. [*1 stroke; margin,* Agreed]

September 6th Granted special warrant against John Walker baker of Shields for defrauding Mr George Wrangham of ditto of his receipt for 7s 6d due from him to the said Wrangham.
[*margin,* Note:] Walker paid all charges. [*circle*]

8th Granted special warrant against Rowland Greenhow of Sunderland pawnbroker for detaining several wareable apparel of Andrew and Merril Craggs of ditto mariner.
N.B. He returned them for common interest. [*1 stroke*]

12<th> Granted general warrant against Sarah Callendar of Shields for leaving the service of Isable Brown salter.
N.B. Dismissed the warrant, Sarah Callendar being sick. [*1 stroke*]

[*page*] 53 *1757*

Affidavits [*three strokes*]

September 16th Granted general warrant upon oath of George Drew of Bishop Wearmouth weaver to search the houses of 4

---

103 I.e. Penshaw.

several persons (whose names are set down) for stolen goods.[104] [2 *strokes*]

18th Granted general warrant against 3 apprentices for deserting the service of Robert Bingham of Sunderland master and mariner. Agreed. [1 *stroke*]

Granted special warrant against Ann Dobson wife of John of Barnsdon constablery for assaulting and striking with a poker etc. William Cummins. Agreed. [*circle*]

19th Granted special warrant against Ann Alexander widow and Margery Watson spinster both of Shields for beating Mary Douglas wife of William Douglas pilot and their daughter. [$2\frac{1}{2}$ *strokes; margin,* Note Ann Alexander paid all charges]

21<st> Granted general warrant against Joseph Hart of Shields weaver for detaining wages for 300 fothars of clay at 3d from William Etherington and Peter Middleton.
Note. Joseph Hart agreed to pay for all, when <*cu*>bed by Mr Merrit. [1 *stroke*]

Granted special warrant against Sarah Stevenson of Sunderland baker for assaulting and bruising Elisabeth Wilson of Durham sempstress and widow. Note: Sarah Stephenson paid all the charges of 5s. [$2\frac{1}{2}$ *strokes*]

Granted special warrant against Elisabeth Waugh and Elisabeth Thompson of Sunderland for receiving the cloaths of Joseph Trotter's wife in pawn (being an hideous drunken creature).
Note: They returned the things again.[105] [1 *stroke*]

[*page*] 54 *1757*

September 24th Granted general warrant against Robert Atkinson

104 Search warrants had to specify clearly whose properties were to be searched, and where: Burn, *The Justice of the Peace*, vol. 3, pp. 226–7.

105 Entry crossed through in black pencil; three blue lines in left margin; 'hideous drunken creature' underlined in blue pencil.

for leaving the service of Francis Scarr of Sunderland master and mariner. [*1 stroke; margin,* Agreed]

26th Granted special warrant against Elisabeth Nicholson (filia populi)[106] for leaving the service of Margery Parker of Sunderland manteau maker. [*1 stroke*]

28<th> Granted general warrant against Thomas Maslett for leaving the service of Robert Bingham of Sunderland master and mariner. Note. Thomas Maslett is a noted perjured youth.[107] [*1 stroke*]

29<th> Granted special warrant against William Crawford of Monk Wearmouth master and mariner for not giving sufficient victuals to his apprentice Thomas Robinson.
Agreed. Not employing him.
That he put him to school etc. [*1 stroke*]

Granted special warrant against Rosamund Mowbray of Bishop Wearmouth for stealing a black coat etc. from George Drew of ditto weaver and offering them to sale to the wife of William Gibson of ditto tanner. Dismissed. [*2 strokes*]

October 4th Wrote to Mrs Smart about turning away her servant Susanna Haslop before the time. [*circle*]

7th Granted general warrant against William Clark of Sunderland miller for detaining £2 2s 9d due for wages to Andrew Davison. [*1 stroke*]

Granted special warrant against Ann Garret wife of William Garret of Monk Wearmouth mariner for assaulting and throwing hot soap sudds upon Elisabeth Bulman wife of George mariner.
Dismissed the warrant Elisabeth Bulman having struck first.[108] [$2\frac{1}{2}$ *strokes*]

---

106 Literally 'daughter of the people', i.e. prostitute.

107 Entry crossed through in black pencil; three blue pencil lines in left margin; 'a noted perjured youth' underlined in blue pencil.

108 Entry crossed through in black pencil; two blue pencil strokes in left margin.

[*page*] 55 *1757*

October 8th Granted special warrant against Peter Jackson of Whitby master and mariner for cruelly using his apprentice Thomas Golightly. [*1 stroke; margin,* Agreed.]

12th Granted special warrant against Alice wife of John Ovingham of Sunderland keelman for bruising Elisabeth [*inserted,* wife of John] Minshon of Shields, and Mary Grundel wife of William Grundel of Shields mariner and taking away William Grundel's handkerchief. [2½ *strokes*]

Granted special warrant against William Donkin of Shields shoemaker for abusing and turning his wife [*inserted,* and children] out of doors, and breaking Isable Hall's window and shutter.
14th Committed for want of sureties by Young, constable. Superseded. [*circle and* 3½ *strokes*]

15th Granted special warrant against Thomas Marshall late of Bishop Wearmouth mariner, upon oath of Ann Brown spinster for begetting a female infant born on old midsummer day last.[109] [*1 stroke*]

17th Granted special warrant against John Robinson of Sunderland mariner for bruising John Mackensye of ditto in the breast. [*1 stroke*]

Passed Elisabeth wife of William Reede of Sunderland mariner and their 2 infants John aged 4 and George 16 months from Shields to Sunderland upon complaint of the overseers. [*3 strokes*]

Margaret Wheatman [*inserted,* of Sunderland] made oath that she is with child by Robert Storey of Monk Wearmouth mariner, from old candlemass night last, or a little after. [*1 stroke*]

---

109 The calendar had been changed in 1752, omitting eleven days, so that 2nd September was followed by 14th September. Midsummer was traditionally 24th June (Feast of John the Baptist), but would later be celebrated on 5th July as the 'old' date: C.R. Cheney, *Handbook of Dates for Students of English History*, Royal Historical Society (London, 1991), pp. 10–11, 154–5; R. Hutton, *The Stations of the Sun: A History of the Ritual Year in Britain* (Oxford, 1996), p. 317.

18th Granted special warrant against Robert [*blank*] of Sunderland master for cruel usage of his apprentice Michael Dryden. [*circle*]

[*page*] 56 *1757*

October 18th Granted special warrant against Christopher Thompson of Monk Wearmouth mariner for bruising and ducking the child of Mary Magham.[110] [*3, or possibly* $2\frac{1}{2}$ *strokes; margin,* Agreed.]

19th Passed Samuel son of John Provand cordwainer from Sunderland to All Saints, Newcastle. [*2 strokes*]

Passed Elizabeth Lyster and her 4 children, the eldest not aged 8, from ditto to St. Nicholas, Newcastle. [*2 strokes*]

Granted special warrant against James Emanuel for leaving the service of Hannah Chilton of Shields at the Fr.[111] boat. [*1 stroke*]

Granted special warrant against Robert Wedderburn for leaving the service of William Blagdon of Shields blacksmith. [*1 stroke*]

21st Granted special warrant against Dorothy Turner of Sunderland widow for detaining <the> wedding ring etc. of the late wife of James Maccron who married her daughter.[112] [*1 stroke*]

24th Gave an order upon the overseer of Hylton constablery to allow John Minnican, wife and 4 small children, 4s per week. [*circle*]

Granted special warrant against Hannah wife of Thomas Pearson of Shields ship-carpenter for breaking the windows etc. of John Walker baker. Agreed. [$2\frac{1}{2}$ *strokes*]

26th Granted special warrant against Francis Watson alias Dove [*inserted,* of Monk Wearmouth, mariner] for assaulting and

---

110 Entry crossed through in black pencil; two blue pencil strokes in left margin; 'bruising and ducking' underlined in blue pencil.

111 I.e. ferry.

112 Entry crossed through in black pencil.

throwing [*inserted*, over] a chest and threatening Stephen Buck, taylor of Monk Wearmouth. [$2\frac{1}{2}$ *strokes*]

[*page*] 57 *1757*

October 31st Granted special warrant against Thomasine and Margaret Mills of Sunderland [*inserted*, spinsters] for bruising Jane Rush of ditto. som.

Gave an Order to the overseers of the poor of Monk Wearmouth to receive a woman and child into their workhouse.

November 1st Granted special warrant against Richard Medcalf of Sunderland skipper for assaulting Mary Thornton widow and her daughter Joanna. sm.

2nd Committed Thomas Maslet to the House of Correction for running away from his master Robert Bingham of Sunderland and not finding sureties. ss. Superseded.

4th Took the deposition of Elisabeth Elliot of Shields spinster that she was ravished on board the Nancy by James Ventris mate thereof on the 2nd instant and that she cryed aloud etc. [*to right* Note: they agreed as I heard at £2 1s 0d][113]

7th Granted general warrant against John Souldbay of Shields joyner for detaining £1 13s 3d due to Thomas Vary mason for wages. s. Agreed.

Granted special warrant against Roger Holyday master and mariner of Monk Wearmouth and Nicholson his put-in-master, for cruelly beating William son of William Scot gardiner to Mrs Gray. N.B. The fact not true and boy ran away to get more wages.[114]

---

113 Note that not all agreements were made in the presence of the justice, nor even reported to him. Entry crossed through in black pencil; two blue pencil strokes in left margin; 'agreed as I heard at £2 1s 0d' underlined in blue pencil.

114 Entry crossed through in black pencil; two blue pencil strokes in left margin.

14th Granted special warrant against Robert Maex of Sunderland shoemaker for assaulting and beating David and June Cowper of ditto labourer. sm. Dismissed.

15th Granted special warrant against Elisabeth Side [*inserted,* widow] for assaulting etc. Jane Rutherforth widow both of Sunderland. sm.

[*page*] 58[115] *1757*

November 17th Granted general warrant against William Fairless of Cleadon labourer for detaining 9s 6d wages from Susan Atkinson.
Note: he payed the wages.

Wrote to Mr J. Cook of Sunderland master to pay a pressed apprentice's wages to his father P. Storer.
Note: J. Cook refused.

Wrote to the overseers of Monk Wearmouth to receive [*blank*] Martin into their workhouse, aged near 80.

19th Granted special warrant against Mac Adys or Edyss of Sunderland barber for beating and burning James Cobb baker of ditto. sm.
Agreed.

21st Granted special warrant against David Stubbs, John Lamb, and Moses Gascarth of Shields labourers for defrauding Robert Noble of Harton of 2s 2d.
Agreed.

Granted special warrant against Jane Mopsey, alias Douglas, for defaming Alice Betson and threatening to fire Jane and Alice Betson wife of William Betson, all of Bishop Wearmouth. sm.
Agreed.

---

115 This is the last page numbered in the manuscript.

22nd Granted general warrant against Peter Wanless of Southwick farmer for detaining £2 12s 6d wages from Thomas Thompson. s.

23rd Settled the difference betwixt Joseph Yellowly of Hylton and servant about wages.

Granted special warrant against Robert Harrison of Sunderland alehousekeeper for inhumanly bruising George Hodge sailor, with 4 others on the 22nd instant. Agreed.

28th Removed Alexander and Catherine Baker from Monk Wearmouth to Sunderland. 3.

December 8th Granted special warrant against William Whitefield of Sunderland mariner for beating bruising and threatening Thomas Dixon of Monk Wearmouth mariner. sm.

[*page* 59] *1757*

December 9th Granted special warrant to the overseer of Monk Wearmouth Shore to relieve Mary Christy and two children.

14th Granted special warrant against Robert Dawes of Bishop Wearmouth salt-maker for turning away from their work Elizabeth and Barbara Johnson. s. Dismissed.

23rd Removed an infant from Shields to All Saints, Newcastle. ss.

Granted order to overseers of the poor of Shields to pay 2s 6d per week to Elisabeth Henderson and her children or to receive them into their workhouse. ss.

24th Granted general warrant against Thomas Sharp of Monk Wearmouth skipper for detaining 4s 6d. wages from James Henderson of Bishop Wearmouth mariner. s.

28th Granted general warrant against Richard Crofton of Sunderland master for refusing to pay £3 wages to John Lindsay his mate.

Granted general warrant against Samuel Tyzack and Robert Thomson apprentices to Mr J. Cookson of Shields for leaving their services. s.[116]

Granted special warrant against Robert Freeman of Cleadon labourer for turning away Martha Albon his servant before her time.
Note: He paid her for her whole time.

[*page* 60] *1758*

January 2nd Granted special warrant against Richard Reay of Shields fisherman for stealing a 3 penny loaf from John Bell servant to John Walker of ditto baker. [*margin,* Not paid]

5th Granted special warrant against William Welch mariner for beating Henry Deans skipper both of Monk Wearmouth. sm. [*margin,* Agreed]

7th Removed Jane Pearson wife of Nicholas, mariner and their 2 children from Monk Wearmouth to Fulwell township.

10th Granted special warrant against John Watson of Shields butcher and farmer for turning away John Richardson from his service. s. [*margin,* Dismissed.]

14th Granted general warrant against Robert Hogg of Whitburn farmer for turning away Margaret Corbet before the expiration of the term. s.

24th Wrote to John Watson of Shields butcher for turning away a maid servant before her time.

25th Granted special warrant against Matthew Jackson of Bishop Wearmouth weaver for bruising Joseph Pool weaver of the same. sm.
N.B. Joseph Pool is a sorry fellow and Matthew Jackson an honest one.

---

116 This J. Cookson of Shields was probably the John Cookson listed in 1760 as owning five salt pans; Hodgson, *The Borough of South Shields*, p. 116.

Granted special warrant against John Williamson of Monk Wearmouth mariner for assaulting and breaking the windows of Robert Pattison of the same alehousekeeper. sm.

30th Granted general warrant against William Crawford master of Monk Wearmouth for detaining £1 10s 0d wages from his apprentice Robert Wood and burning his indentures. s.

[There are no entries for February – May 1758.]

[*page* 61] *1758*

June 9th Granted special warrant against John Cam of Shields officer in the salt duties for a gun several times to affright the horse of Francis Anderson labourer then leading water. sm. [*margin,* Agreed at 4s 6d.][117]

10th Granted general warrant against Amos Hedley a soldier of Shields for assaulting etc. John Kell of ditto miller. sm. [*margin,* Agreed.]

Granted general warrant against Joseph Greenwell late of Sunderland butcher for detaining 15s 6d wages from Lucy Hyslop. s.

12<th> Granted special warrant against Ann Taylor of Sunderland spinster for endeavouring to stab with a spit John Fleming her fellow servant. sm.[118]

16th Granted special summons to Archibald Campbell of Monk Wearmouth barber to answer his apprentice Robert Love<'s> complaint of want of victuals. s.
Agreed and the master paid the charges.

19th Granted general warrant against Percival Hall of Monk Wearmouth Shore blacksmith for detaining wages from Ralph Blakiston. s.

---

117 Entry crossed through in black pencil; three blue pencil strokes in left margin.
118 Entry crossed through in black pencil; one blue pencil stroke in left margin.

22nd Granted special warrant against Jonathan Somers of Shields glassman for beating and bruising Ann Hodge and her son Cuthbert Hodge with a thick stick. sm. Agreed.

26th Granted special warrant against Isable wife of Richard Hallifax of Monk Wearmouth mariner for threatening the life of Thomas Watson of ditto mariner, and to stone him wherever she met him. sm. Agreed.

Granted special warrant against [*blank*] apprentice to Mr James Smithson of Monk Wearmouth for deserting his service.

[*page* 62] *1758*

June 29th Granted general warrant to the overseer of Westo to take up Richard Gibson for leaving his wife and child. s.

Granted special warrant to Ann Younghusband of Shields salter against [*blank*] for leaving her service. s. [*margin*, Discharged.]

Granted special warrant to J. Jefferson of Harton against Richard Reay pilot for throwing down his milk and beating the maid. ss.

July 1st Granted special s.[119] warrant against Jane wife of William Rutter of Shields for charging Isable Hall widow with carrying away wort from Mr Grainger's mashfat. sm.
Agreed, if Jane Rutter pays 3s 6d. in a fortnight's time.[120]

4th Granted special warrant against Nicholas Byars of Bishop Wearmouth farmer for beating and bruising William Clark of Sunderland miller. sm.
Dismissed.

11th Granted special warrant against Elisabeth wife of John Robson of Sunderland mariner for cutting the nose and lip of Jane Newton wife of [*blank*] Newton sailor of the same.
sm. Agreed at 16s.

---

119 Summons?

120 Entry crossed through in black pencil; two blue pencil strokes in left margin.

14th Granted general warrant against Samuel Carter of Sunderland master and mariner for not paying to Thomas Gibson his apprentice £3 5s 0d wages. s.
Agreed.

14th Granted special warrant against William Matthew tanner for beating Thomas Hall of Boldon carpenter and threatening to set fire to his coals. sm. Agreed.[121]

26th Granted special warrant against James Morris of Shields salter for beating and threatening Thomas Ouston a blind man and salter and also beating Isable Rushwood widow both of Shields.
Not paid.

[*page* 63] *1758*

July 26th Transferred the licence of Granthem Harper of Shields to John Chilton late master and mariner of good character. s.

28th Granted special warrant against Robert Thompson of Sunderland keelman and Elisabeth his wife for beating and bruising in many secret parts Ann Rushworth of the same widow. sm. [*margin,* Agreed at 11s 6d.]

Wrote to Mr William Rockwood [*inserted,* of Shields] to pay John Scot apprentice to Robert Cummin master and mariner half his wages due for the last voyage with him, the said Scot being deserted by his master and having no manner of provision appointed for him. o.

31st Granted special warrant against James Tate boatman for refusing to land George Holmes salt-officer at Shields and abusing him and t<e>aring his cloaths. s.[122]

---

121 For William Matthew, tanner, see the earlier drunkenness offence on July 13th 1752, connected with his presumed relative Richard; they came before the quarter sessions: DRO, Q/S/OB 11, p. 111.

122 Entry crossed through in black pencil; two blue pencil strokes in left margin.

August 1st Margaret Hunter of Silksworth in Bishop Wearmouth made oath that she is now pregnant with child and that John Moore of the same batchelor is the father. s.
Granted warrant against the said John Moore.

3rd Granted special warrant against Robert Wishart for beating and threatening Robert Lamb of Sunderland porter. sm.

Granted general warrant against Ralph Bolton of Shields keelman and a common drunkard for threatening the life of Mary Dixon wife of Simon, mariner. sm.

[*page* 64] *1758*

August 3rd Granted special warrant against Alice wife of James Steward of Shields labourer for beating and trampling on the belly of Mary wife of Thomas Capeling of ditto shoemaker. sm.[123]

4th Granted general warrant against Mary Wood [*inserted*, of Southwick] for leaving the service of Samuel Ather of Hart farmer. s.
Agreed upon Mary Wood's paying a quarter's wages and charges in all 15s.

10th Granted special warrant against Jane wife of Michael Crow of Sunderland labourer for beating and threatening Margaret Walker of the same. sm.

17th Granted general warrant against George Trumball for assaulting and dragging down stairs Elisabeth Porter [*inserted*, wife of John Porter] both of the township of Berkley, pitmen. sm.

18th Granted special warrant against Mary Todd of Monk Wearmouth spinster for breaking the hedges of Mr George Longstaff, upon the oath of Robert Richardson. o.

Granted general warrant against Robert Wedderburn of Shields labourer for bruising and beating Ann Harper and her daughter

123 Entry crossed through in black pencil; two blue pencil strokes in left margin.

Christiana Sharp both of the same. sm. [*margin*, Dismissed] – the mother and daughter both bad.

21st Granted general warrant against William Jeffray miller for leaving the service of George Reay of Sunderland miller. s [*margin*, Dismissed.]

[*page* 65] *1758*

23rd Granted general warrant against John Brown of Monk Wearmouth master and mariner for detaining £7 wages from Anthony Baker his apprentice. s.

Granted general warrant against Mary Blair of Shields fruiterer for beating and bruising upon the head Ann Bone of the same widow. sm.

August 28th Granted special warrant against Adam Davidson of Monk Wearmouth roper for beating and bruising William Loggan labourer. sm. [*margin*, Due 1s.]

Granted general warrant against James Richardson keelman and Ann his wife for threatening the life of Margaret wife of Robert Atkinson keelman and their children, of Sunderland. sm.
Agreed upon paying charges.

29th Wrote to Mr M. Burleigh to settle a debt of <£>2 8<s> 0<d> claimed by Jane Hawkinson for her husband William's wages from George Sympson [*inserted*, one] of Mr Burleigh's masters.

Granted special warrant against Ann wife of James Wardall of Sunderland shoemaker for instigating a child (Joanna Carter) to steal shoes for her which she received. sm.
A summons also for Mary Murray witness.

September 1st Granted general warrant against Elinor wife of John Anderson of Shields trimmer for beating and bruising Jane wife of William Rutter of ditto. sm.
[*margin*, Agreed to pay half]

5th Granted general warrant against John Thompson for leaving the service of Edward Browel now of Monk Wearmouth master and mariner. s.

9th Granted special warrant against Elisabeth wife of John Thompson of Sunderland porter for threatening the life of Mary Sharp of the same widow. sm.

[*page* 66] *1758*

September 12th Granted special warrant against Thomas Richardson of Shields blacksmith for threatening Jane Skipsey of the Laygate widow. sm.

16th Granted special warrant against Dorothy wife of Hugh Cow of Shields salter for threatening the lives of Frances and Rachel Brown of ditto salters. sm. [*margin,* Agreed]

25th Granted general warrant against Thomas Golightly for leaving the service of Robert Turner of Bishop Wearmouth master and mariner, and a summons against John Softley of Sunderland master for detaining and imploying him. s. [*margin,* Agreed]

26th Granted special warrant against William Grainger of Shields pilot for beating Ralph Purviss of ditto pilot. sm. [*margin,* Agreed at 7s 6d]

29th Granted special warrant against Robert Harrison of Sunderland trimmer for beating Robert [*blank*] of ditto coalseller. sm. [*margin,* Agreed at 7s.]

Granted special warrant against Ann Doe, or Dough of Sunderland, widow for bruising the body and t<e>aring of the hair etc. of Elisabeth Campbell wife of Dennis Campbell of ditto mariner. sm. [*margin,* Agreed at 5s]

October 2nd Took the deposition of Sarah Colson of Sunderland spinster, that she is now with child by Robert Bellaby of ditto grocer. s.

[*page* 67] *1758*

October 2nd Granted special warrant against Edward Wear [*inserted,* saltmaker] Isable his wife and 2 daughters [*inserted,* all of Shields] for assaulting and beating etc. William Moor of ditto keelman.

7th Granted general warrant against James Moore for not paying 7s. 6d to William Morriss both of Shields. s.

19th Granted special warrant against Mary Blair of Shields widow for stealing a peice of white cloth value 2s. 7d from the house of George Irons of ditto labourer. sm.

Granted special warrant to the constable of Whitburn to summon William Harkass overseer to appear before me [*inserted,* on the 23rd] and shew cause why relief should not be given to Mary Leighton. o.

20th Granted special warrant against Robert and Sarah Gaskard of Shields salters for wounding etc. Dorothy Mackay of ditto salter. sm.
Agreed at 5s.

23<rd> Granted special warrant against Thomas Turner of Shields labourer for kicking on the belly Mary wife of Joseph Grant of ditto labourer. sm.
Agreed at 8s.[124]

Sent summons warrant to John [*blank*] overseer of Jarro to show cause why Susan Henderson should not be relieved. o.

26th Granted special warrant against Hannah Menham wife of Thomas, potmaker of Shields, for turning away her servant Bridget Adams, striking her with an iron poker and bruising her. s.
Agreed to pay all.

---

124 Two blue pencil strokes in left margin.

[*page* 68] *1758*

October 30th Granted special warrant against Mary Baker of Monk Wearmouth singlewoman for refusing to tell the father of her bastard child to the overseer George Bryan. s.

November 2nd Took the deposition of Robert Henderson of Jarro labourer that his late brother John was born at Welton in the parish of Ovingham in Northumberland and thereupon removed his wife Susanna a lunatic, and Robert their son to the township of Welton aforesaid. sss.

22nd Granted general warrant against Robert Robson of Southwick farmer for detaining £2 2s 9d from his servant Stephen Ayre. s.

25th Granted general warrant against William Atkinson of Monk Wearmouth for knocking down David Marshall one of the wherryboatmen, so that his life is despaired of, as Daniel Brown shoemaker of Sunderland deposes on oath.
[*margin*, Agreed (as I hear) at £5][125]

December 11th Granted special warrant against Jonathan Hutchinson of the parish of Jarro miller and joyner for bruising and threatening John Dixon of the same, taylor. sm.

14th Summoned the overseers of Whitburn to answer the complaint of [*blank*] Herriot, master of the workhouse for not paying for the provision of the poor, as agreed. s.

15th Granted special warrant against William Whitfield mariner of Sunderland for beating and bruising John Bingham ditto of ditto. sm.

[*page* 69] *1758 & 1759*

December 22nd Granted summons warrant against John Taylor of Monk Wearmouth master and mariner for shooting and taking up Mrs Grey's pidgeons. o.

---

125 Another instance of an agreement only indirectly reported to Tew.

30th Granted special warrant against James Birkley and Richard Reay of Shields for assaulting and beating Charles Gray pilot. sm.

Took the deposition of Simon Hutchinson master and mariner. o.

1759

January 2nd Granted general warrant against James Farrar for leaving the service of John Fairless of Shields, master and mariner. s.

2nd Removed William Dodds and Jane his wife from Whitburn to Morton in the Whins in Dalton [*inserted,* le Dale] parish. ss.

3rd Committed James Birkley and Richard Reay to goal for want of securities. Superseded.

15th Granted 3 general warrants against 3 apprentices for running away from 3 different ships, belonging to Adam Bowlby Esq. of Whitby master. sss.

Granted warrant against William Hogget of Monk Wearmouth baker for stealing and breaking up the boat of Thomas Wood of Bishop Wearmouth keelman. sm.

16th Committed William Hogget to the county goal. ss.
Superseded.

[*page* 70] *1759*

January 17th Granted general warrant against John Bee for deserting the service of Robert Sabron of Sunderland master and mariner. ss.

19th Granted special warrant against Anthony Thompson of Monk Wearmouth keelman for bruising and breaking the collar bone of Francis Howe of ditto skipper. sm.
Note Francis Howe struck first and paid all charges.

22nd Granted general warrant against John Ford of Sunderland mariner for stealing the boat etc. of Matthew Cook of Bishop Wearmouth. sm.

Granted special warrant against Abraham Smith, Lancelot Smith of Sunderland butchers and Thomas Atkinson of Bishop Wearmouth butcher for beating and bruising George Bryce of Sunderland butcher. sm.

24th Granted special warrant against John Chance etc. for running away with the boat of Matthew Cook of Bishop Wearmouth. s.

25th Summoned the overseer of Southwick to shew cause why Elinor Lonsdale and daughter should not be relieved. o.
He appeared, and I ordered them 1s per week.

February 2nd Granted special warrant against Thomas Facton of Shields ballast-heaver for bruising James Morriss of ditto saltmaker. sm.

3rd Granted summons warrant against Percival Hall of Monk Wearmouth blacksmith for turning away his servantmaid Margaret Law. s.
Dismissed the warrant, Margaret Law being a false impudent woman.

[*page* 71] *1759*

February 3rd Granted special warrant against Margaret wife of John Smith of Bishop Wearmouth borer for assaulting etc. Elinor Short wife of Robert Short of ditto blacksmith. sm.

Granted special warrant against Isable Young widow of Shields salter for assaulting and t<e>aring of the gown of Ann Henderson of ditto spinster, and breaking the windows of her landlady. sm.

12th Granted special warrant against Margaret Roxby widow and Elisabeth Swan spinster both of Monk Wearmouth for knocking down Margaret Purviss spinster of ditto. sm.
Mem. Bound them over – released. sss4.

Granted special warrant against James Bainbridge of Whitburn for leaving the service of his master. s.
N.B. He returned to him.

Granted special warrant against John Buck apprentice for leaving the service of his master Archibald Campbell of Monk Wearmouth barber. s.
Mem. I bound them over.

14<th> Granted special warrant against John Stevenson of Shields schoolmaster for charging William Shields musicmaster with a robbery of £6 in gold and silver out of his desk. sm.
Agreed.

15th Granted special warrant against John Hutchinson alehousekeeper and Elinor his wife of Sunderland for beating Daniel Makemirth weaver of ditto. sm.

Thomas Elliot made oath that he served the last year's service with John Merriman blacksmith of Hylton constablery. o.

Anthony Wood of Boldon to ditto. s.

[*page* 72] *1759*

February 15th Wrote to William Forsyth of Sheilds to mend the windows of Mary Hathoway which he has broken. o.

23rd Granted general warrant against Matthew Cook of Bishop Wearmouth mason and boatman for cruel usage of his wife. so.

Granted special warrant to Thomas Sellars gentleman and William [*blank*] boat builder of Shields to be bread weighers and inspectors into meal of all grains for the said town of Shields and swore them both into their office. sss.[126]

---

126 Magistrates had a duty to appoint 'clerks of the market' to view the sale of any meal or grain, and make sure that bread was being sold at the weight and price set by the mayor or any two justices locally: Burn, *The Justice of the Peace*, 5th edition, 1758, pp. 95–8. Entry crossed through in black pencil; one blue pencil stroke in left margin.

27th Granted 2 special warrants against James Robinson of Sunderland master and mariner for cruelly beating and knocking out the teeth of 2 apprentices. ss.[127]

Granted special warrant against Joanna Allen of Westo widow for charging William Bates of ditto with stealing a green purse of gold and cocks and hens. sm.[128]

Granted special warrant against Thomas Dixon of Shields lighterman for stealing a cock from Thomas Leighton of Westo cobler, the property of Jacob Adesmith. sm.

28th Granted special warrant against [*blank*] Stoddard and John Embledon of Monk Wearmouth for running a cart into the River Wear the property of William Reay ballastmaker of Sunderland. s.[129]

[*page* 73] *1759*

March 2nd Granted special warrant against Bridget Adams of Shields spinster for stealing out of the house of her master Hugh Wishaw salt officer, caps, ruffles, hankerchiefs and soap, of the value of 10s, being his property. ss.

3rd Granted special warrant against George Denham of Monk Wearmouth rope and rag merchant for assaulting and bruising John Parker of ditto shoemaker. sm.
Agreed.

5th Granted general warrant against John Edwards of Monk Wearmouth shipwright for assaulting James Dicks of ditto shipwright and dragging him through the dirt. sm.
Agreed at 6s.

6th Granted general warrant against Richard Hall apprentice to John Marshall of Scarborough master and mariner for leaving his services.

---

127 Entry crossed through in black pencil; one blue pencil stroke in left margin.
128 Entry crossed through in black pencil.
129 Entry crossed through in black pencil; one blue pencil stroke in left margin.

Granted general warrant against Sarah Callendar [*inserted*, saltmaker] for assaulting and bruising Esther Cousin wife of Anthony Cousin keelman and Esther their daughter all of Shields. sm. [*margin*, Agreed]

9th Took the deposition of Elisabeth Harper of Whitburn spinster, that she is with child by Joseph Sheville of Boldon mariner, against whom (at the request of the overseer of Whitburn) I granted a warrant. sm.

[*page* 74] *1759*

March 17th Granted special warrant against William Liversage or Liverstitch of Monk Wearmouth keelman for threatening Susanna Crow and charging her and Robert Crow her husband of ditto with opening the barn and stealing corn, of Mr J. Stafford of ditto farmer. sm.

23rd Granted special warrant against Hannah Menham of Shields for cruelly beating, biting and bruising on the breast Elisabeth Colville her servant. sm.
Agreed for a guinea.[130]

April 7th Granted general warrant against Mary Blair of Shields widow for beating and bruising Isable Reed of ditto, spinster. sm.

9th Granted special warrant against James and Jane Turner of Sunderland mason for beating Grace wife of Thomas Clifford a soldier. sm.

10th Wrote a letter to Captain Arnold Jackson of South Shields of his wife's offering to make affidavit of her innocency. o.[131]

17th Signed a protection. s. Another. s.

---

130 Entry crossed through in black pencil; two blue pencil strokes in left margin; 'a guinea' underlined in blue pencil.
131 Two blue pencil strokes in left margin.

19th Wrote to John Lonsdale about the vile behaviour of his wife, and to make amends to Walter Davison's wife. o.[132]

Sent a warrant to the constable and overseer of Westo to allow 1s per week to widow Ann Clark aged 67. o.

Sent summons warrant to the overseers of Whitburn to pay James Herriot for keeping their poor. s.

20<th> Bound over William Harkas to appear at the sessions in the sum of £10. sm. Withdrawn.

[*page* 75] *1759*

Granted general warrant against William Clark of Shields miller for not paying 8s to Percival Hall for wages. s.

May 1st Granted special warrant against Thomas Addison mate of the Mayflower, Joseph Jefferson of Monk Wearmouth commander, for beating and threatening James Vandermass his apprentice etc. sm.

3rd Granted general warrant to [*sic*] John Younghusband of Shields saltmaker for detaining 9s 4d from Margery and Ann Brown. s.

Granted summons warrant against Christopher Lyddel of Westo farmer to show cause why he refuses to be constable for Westo. s.

7th Granted general warrant against Andrew Melvin of Gateshead nailer upon the oath of Anna Buteling that she is with child by him. ss.

Granted general warrant against Martin Pattison of Monk Wearmouth master and mariner for detaining £5 for labour on board of the Two Brothers from Alexander Christy of ditto. s.
Agreed at £4 10s 0d.

---

132 Two blue pencil strokes in left margin.

14<th> Granted special warrant against Christ.[133] Dysen a soldier's wife of Shields for bruising etc. Sarah Robson of ditto baker. sm.

Granted general warrant against John Robson for leaving the service of John Wood of Boldon farmer. s.

16th Granted special warrant against William Todd of Monk Wearmouth [*inserted,* carpenter] and Elisabeth Todd of ditto for beating etc. Mary wife of William Locksmith of ditto master and mariner. sm.

[*page* 76] *1759*

May 17th Granted general warrant against Jane Ross servant to Elisabeth Brewster of Hedworth widow for feloniously carrying away 3 gowns, 5 shirts, a guinea, and 1s 6d. o.

Granted search warrant for the entring the house and mill of Thomas Bartram of Monkton Mill, an apron of the said Brewster being found with the maid Elisabeth Fail. o. [*inserted,* N.B.] Nothing proved against Fail.

Granted general warrant against James Young of Shields shopkeeper for deserting his wife etc. s.

18th Granted special warrant against Nicholas Swan mariner (of a press gang) for violently bruising Deborah Hartley [*inserted,* alias Arkley] upon head and breasts. sm.[134]

Affidavits [*4 strokes*]

23rd Granted special warrant against Mary Blair [*inserted,* alias Weldon fruiterer] for beating and threatening Isable Reed of Shields spinster and throwing into the mill dam, her potatoes and beatment. sm.
N.B. Both are very bad women.

---

133 I.e. Christiana or a variant.

134 Nicholas Swan was fined £5 and sentenced to remain in gaol until it was paid: DRO, Q/S/OB 12, p.15.

24th Committed her to the House of Correction for want of sureties. o. Superseded.

26th Granted special warrant against Robert Brown of Sunderland skipper for bruising William Fleming of Bishop Wearmouth boatman. sm.

Granted special warrant against Barbara Anderson of Monk Wearmouth milkseller for knocking out 2 teeth of Ann wife of Matthew Cook of Bishop Wearmouth. sm. Agreed at 14s.

[*page* 77] *1759*

May 30th Granted special warrant against Timothy Gray of Monk Wearmouth master for abusing Thomas Hedley apprentice of Edward Hutchinson of ditto master. s.

June 7th Granted general warrant against Richard Anthony for leaving the service of Lancelot Charlton of Shields brickmaker. s.

Granted special warrant against Miles Hudson of Shields labourer for beating Ruth wife of George Snaith of ditto blacksmith now with child. sm.

Granted general warrant against William Mills hired to Thomas Young of Boldon farmer for not coming to his place. s.
Mem. He came to his place.

12<th> Granted general warrant against Henry Bramber apprentice to Paul Carter of Sunderland shoemaker for refusing to work, though in perfect health. s.

14th Committed Nicholas Swan to goal for want of securities. s.

15th Granted special warrant against William Kelsey the elder of Shields pilot for assaulting and threatening Richard Hylton of ditto joyner.

16th Granted special warrant against [*blank*] Robson of Monk Wearmouth hatter for beating and bruising Thomas Burdon of ditto trimmer. sm.

18th Margaret Fleet of Monk Wearmouth spinster swore a bastard to Robert Smith mariner *deceased,* from 1st January. s.

Granted summons warrant against the overseers of Whitburn about 3 infants (called Kay) being not provided for. s.

[*page* 78] *1759*

June 20th Granted special warrant against Archibald Boey for knocking down and bruising William Maxwell boatman of Shields. sm.

Granted special warrant against William (called the Londoner) for abusing and attempting to lye with Sarah Paget of Shields widow (about 45) and stealing her handkercheif. sm.[135] [*margin,* Not found]

22nd Granted special warrant against Alice wife of Joseph Harper of Westo farmer for breaking the window of Robert Harper and ill treating his wife Ann. sm.

25th Granted special warrant against Robert Glover of Shields butcher for breaking the windows and beating William Gibson of Shields butcher. sm. [*margin,* Dismissed.]

Made a mittimus for Archibald Boey. ss.
Superseded.

27th Granted general warrant against Mary Cole for leaving the service of George Crofton of Jarro farmer. s. [*margin, Note* she returned]

July 2nd Granted special warrant against William Moore, Ralph Moore and Anthony Cousins of Shields keelmen for beating and bruising Hugh and Dorothy Mackay saltmakers. sm.
Agreed at a guinea – but they [*inserted,* are] all bad impudent people, and would not pay the guinea.[136]

---

135 Two black and two blue pencil strokes in left margin.
136 Two blue pencil strokes in left margin.

Wrote to Mrs Smart for beating and turning away her maid. o.[137]

July 6th Granted peace warrant against Janet Kidd wife of James Kidd of Monk Wearmouth labourer for threatening the life of Jane wife of Gavin Argo of ditto labourer. sm.

[*page* 79] *1759*

July 9th Granted special warrant against Robert Husband of Shields keelman and Mary his wife for breaking the windows etc. of Elisabeth Brown saltmaker. sm. Agreed.

Granted general warrant against William Crawford of Monk Wearmouth master and mariner for detaining £7 from his apprentice – James Jurdoson. s.

11th Granted special warrant against James Dykes of Monk Wearmouth carpenter for beating and knocking down Thomas Wilkinson of Sunderland boatman. sm.

14th Committed William Moore, Ralph Moore and Anthony Cousins [*inserted*, all of Shields keelmen], to goal, for want of sufficient sureties. ss.

15th Committed William Matthew of West Boldon tanner to goal, upon complaint of Edward Softley against him, for want of sufficient sureties. o.

17th Granted special warrant against Katherine wife of [*blank*] Tinmouth pilot, and Katherine their daughter for throwing mire and dirt and a tub full of water upon Isable wife of Thomas Young cobleman, all of Shields. sm.
Agreed upon paying charges.

18th Granted special warrant against William and John Berkley of Shields bakers for beating and bruising Hannah Prisek of ditto. sm.
Run away.

---

137 Two blue pencil strokes in left margin continued down from the entry above.

20th Granted special warrant against Margaret Holmes wife of Richard of Monk Wearmouth trimmer for bruising and threatening Ann wife of Thomas Farley of ditto skipper. sm. Agreed.

[*page* 80] *1759*

July 21st Passed 3 infants Ann, George and Margaret Kay children of George Kay or Cay late of Whitburn deceased to Scarborough in Yorkshire. ss.

24th Wrote to Symon Miller of Shields taylor to deliver up a coat intrusted with him to Mary Rochester of ditto. o.

Passed Hannah widow of Thomas Atkinson labourer deceased together with 4 infants from Monk Wearmouth to Pelton township in the parish of Chester-le-Street. ss.

25th Granted special warrant against Alice wife of Joseph Harper of Westo farmer for bruising Peter Hedley labourer with a fork etc. sm.

Wrote to John Rutter of Shields blacksmith for abusing Thomas Mills constable. o.

Bound over Alice wife of Joseph Harper to appear at the next sessions, Joseph Harper farmer in £20 and William Hedley carpenter in £20. sss4. Superseded.

28th Granted special warrant against Robert Revel of Sunderland cobleman for throwing peices of wood against Elisabeth wife of Robert Thompson of ditto keelman and threatening her life. sm. Agreed at 10s 6d and charges 3s 6d.

30th Granted general warrant against Wardal Wainman of Sunderland keelman for getting Mary Todd of Monk Wearmouth (a common strumpet) with child, who hath this day sworn it to him. ss.

[*page* 81] *1759*

August 3rd Granted special warrant against John Henzell of Shields brickmaker for snatching a guinea from John Banks of ditto exciseman. s. Agreed.

4th Granted general warrant against Richard Adams of Shields glassman for getting Hannah Douglas of ditto singlewoman with child, who hath this day sworn it to him. ss.

6th Granted special warrant against Jane Bilton [*inserted*, of Sunderland] for assaulting Joanna Bamborough of Sunderland brickmaker etc. sm.

Granted special warrant against Thomas Pearson of Shields butcher for not instructing his apprentice Robert Lumsdon now being in his last year in the mystery of his trade. s.

7th Granted general warrant against William Raphael or Raffel of Great Usworth waggon man, for bruissing [*sic*] etc. his brother Francis of ditto, ditto. sm.

11th Granted general warrant against Stephen Grieves apprentice for leaving the service of Timothy Gray of Monk Wearmouth master and mariner. s.

Passed James Richey aged near 6, son of James Richey a disbanded soldier who deceased within the parish of Whitburn, from Monk Wearmouth Shoreside to Whitburn. ss. Passed also the mother Barbara Richey. ss.

21st Granted special warrant against John Coundon and J. Wood keelman of Sunderland for defrauding the Pan boatman of his dues. s.

Affidavits [*9 strokes*]

[*page* 82] *1759*

August 23rd Granted special warrant against Jonathan Somers of Shields glassmaker for throwing a tea kettle of hot water against the servant of William Grainger of ditto innholder. sm. [*margin*, Agreed.]

September 1st Granted general warrant against [*blank*] for throwing Matthew Robinson of the Shore apprentice overboard. sm.

3rd Granted general warrant against Philip Dowsey of Bishop Wearmouth carpenter for breaking open a box and stealing from thence a will and a bond of £20 etc. the property of Elisabeth Knockles of Monk Wearmouth widow. sm.

Summoned overseer of Monk Wearmouth to provide for Isable wife of Ralph Wilkinson and children. o.

Granted general warrant against Abraham Brown of Shields skipper for running away with the keel of James Moore of ditto. s. [*margin*, Dismissed.]

5th Granted general warrant against Robert Herbert for leaving the service of Isaac Kirton of North Shields sailmaker. s.

10th Granted general warrant against Jane Gibson for leaving the service of Richard Fawel of Wardley farmer. s.

13th Granted general warrant against Sarah Fisher of Shields spinster for beating with a stone Jane wife of George Nelson salt officer, so that she lay for *dead*. sm.[138] [*margin*, Dismissed.]

17th Granted special warrant against Elisabeth Specks and Isable wife and daughter of Cuthbert Specks mariner of Sunderland for bruising etc. Ann wife of Richard Thomlinson of ditto shipcarpenter. sm.

[*page* 83] *1759*

Affidavits [*6 strokes*]

September 17th Granted special warrant against Jane Nelson wife

138 Entry crossed through in black pencil; two blue pencil strokes in left margin.

of George salt officer in Shields for bruising and assaulting with a case knife Thomas and Jane Pye of ditto shipwright. sm. Agreed at 7<s>. 6<d>.

24th Granted special warrant against Mary Blair alias Weldon of Shields fruiterer for beating and threatening Sarah Precise of ditto widow, and Margaret Harrison of ditto washerwoman. sm.

October 5th Granted special warrant against Robert Rogerson of Gateshead Fell quarryman for bruising etc. Jane Burton wife of Francis of Jarro labourer. sm. Agreed at 15s.

10th Granted general warrant against George Rippon of Shields brickmaker for refusing to pay 4s to 2 children of [*blank*] Harding of ditto for work. s.

12th Granted general warrant against Jane Thompson [*inserted*, a common strumpet] for refusing to pay George Drew master of Bishop Wearmouth workhouse three shillings for labour. s.

13th Granted special warrant against Edward Proctor of Monk Wearmouth mariner for running away with the boat of Matthew Cook of Sunderland boatman. sm.

15th Granted general warrant against Thomas Wilson of Sunderland keelman for threatening John Hall bailiff to the commissioners of Wear etc. o.[139]

16th Granted general warrant against Jane Rogers, and Ann Sympson of Shields salters for leaving the service of John Mackguy saltmaker. s.

18th Took the examination of Barbara Hayton and granted general warrant against John son of Thomas Davison of Sunderland taylor for felony. sm.

139 The Wear Commissioners were the body responsible for the re-shaping of the River Wear in Sunderland: S. Miller (ed.), *The River Wear Commissioners: Extracts from their Papers, 1717–1846*, Durham County Local History Society, Documentary Series 3 (Durham, 1980).

[*page* 84] *1759*

October 22nd 1759 Granted general warrant against Margaret and Ann Brown of Shields salters for leaving the service of Robert Brown their master. s.

24th Granted general peace warrant against Jane wife of [*blank*] Monk Wearmouth taylor for threatening the life of Rachel Bell servant of Mr Thomas Dixon of ditto fitter. o.

[There are no entries for November 1759.]

December 27th Granted general warrant against Mary Burn wife of James Burn of Sunderland alehousekeeper for bruising Ann White wife of James White maltmaker of ditto. sm.

Granted general warrant against Robert Rockwood of Shields mariner for getting with child Margaret Anderson spinster of which she was delivered on the 26th November 1759. sm.

Granted special warrant against John Baird of Shields boatbuilder for flinging down and cutting upon the eye James Henderson of Simyside[140] blacksmith. sm. Agreed at 15s.

[*page* 85] *1760* [*1½ strokes*]

January 10th Wrote to the overseer of Great Usworth to relieve Margaret Lander widow and to appear on the 12th.

11th Granted general warrant against William Thompson of Sunderland mate for wantonly beating and bruising William Hartley and James Gowland. sm. Agreed upon Thompson paying charges.

Granted special warrant against David Henderson and Samuel Athra alias Arthur, of Monk Wearmouth servants for whipping with a whin-bush upon her legs and thighs Jane Fletcher their fellow servant. ss. Agreed at £1 1s 0d.

---

140 I.e. Simonside.

14th Granted special warrant against Alice wife of Joseph Harper of Shields farmer for bruising with a poker John Robson her hired servant. s.

15th Granted special warrant against Thomas Taylor and another of Jarro labourers for beating and bruising George Robson of Carrs Hill miller. sm. Dismissed.

16th Ann Gambsby swore herself with child by William Hardy of Sunderland shoemaker. s.

17th Wrote to Mrs Jackson of Shields about her husband's quarrel with her. o.

Wrote to Whitburn overseers about Hannah Martin. o.

22nd Granted special warrant against Gibson Gray of Sunderland keelman for taking away the good name and fame of Elisabeth Adams of Monk Wearmouth and charging her with whoredom etc. s.[141]

Granted special warrant against John Simey of Washington labourer for beating and bruising Samuel Dove of ditto labourer. sm.

[*page* 86] *1760*

January 24th Wrote to John Chilton of Shields pilot about turning away his servant Isable Thompson. o.

26th Granted special warrant against John Storey of Bishop Wearmouth farmer for refusing to pay the wages due to two of his milksellers living at Sunderland. o.

Granted special warrant against Elisabeth wife of John Purdey of Monk Wearmouth labourer for threatening the life of Jane wife of George Allison of ditto trimmer. sm.
Dismissed.

---

141 Entry crossed through in black pencil; four blue pencil strokes in left margin.

28th Granted special warrant against James Walker, barber, Robert Barras salt officer, and Joseph Thompson postman of Shields for a riot at the house of Mary wife of John Paul innholder of ditto. sm.

Removed William Haswell ballast heaver from Monk Wearmouth Shore to township of Middle Herrington in the parish of Houghton-le-Spring, Durham. ss.

Margaret Fenwick [*inserted*, of Bell Key Jarro] swore a bastard to Mr Newark Hudson of Sunderland fitter. s.

Granted general warrant against Thomas Dunn of Sunderland mariner for feloniously stealing his own note of hand for £4 14s 0d payable upon demand to Thomas Rennison of ditto Sunderland innholder. sm.

Removed Elisabeth wife of William Loggan Scotchman and John Loggan their child from Monk Wearmouth Shore to Sunderland. ss.

[*page 87*] *1760*

January 29th Granted general warrant against Mary wife of Thomas Copeland of Shields shoemaker for making a riot about the house of Grantham Harper of ditto butcher at ten of the clock – when the family were in bed. sm.

30th Bound over Robert Barras salt-officer in £20, John Cam ditto in £10, and John Overend ditto in £10 for Robert Barras's appearance at the quarter sessions, to answer Mary wife of John Paul, for bursting open her door, breaking her windows, beating and bruising her betwixt 12 and 1 at night on the 26th and 27th January. sssm.[142]

February 6th Granted general warrant against Ann wife of

---

142 In fact, Mary and John Paul, with Thomas Lee, were fined for assaulting Robert Barras, rather than the reverse, Mary Paul £5, and the others 1s: DRO, Q/S/OB 12, p.45, 16 October 1760.

Thomas Wardal of Sunderland shoemaker for bruising Margaret Oliver of ditto. sm.

11th Granted general warrant against Ralph Ellison of Shields shoemaker for feloniously seizing and carrying away a silk handkerchief value 2s from the neck of Sarah Oliver of ditto spinster. sm.

12th Wrote to Mr Nicholas Fairless of Shields for cruelly beating Elizabeth Grierson of ditto. o.[143]

Wrote also to Captain John Taylor of Monk Wearmouth Green to take again his neice (whom his brother left to his charge and with whom he had £20) who was returned to Peter Johnson of Monk Wearmouth sawyer who marryed the girl's mother. Note: the girl is next to an ideot. o.[144]

[*page* 88] *1760*

February 12th Granted special warrant against John Annesley, Thomas Carr, James Taylor [*inserted*, taylor] Mrs [*blank*] Cheshire and Mrs [*blank*] Smith, all of Sunderland slopsellers and unlicensed pawnbrokers for receiving, shirts, wastcoast [*sic*], sets of delft, handkerchief etc. the goods of John Ovington of Bishop Wearmouth shipwright. sm. Agreed at 8s and returning the goods.

13th Transferred the license of Mrs Ann Pickering of Monk Wearmouth widow to Archibald Purviss of ditto who hath taken her house. ss.

18th Granted special warrant against John Stephenson of Berkely pitman for beating and t<e>aring the coat and threatening the life of William Middleton of ditto pitman. sm.

---

143 Nicholas Fairless, father of the man of the same name murdered in 1832, was an important lessee of land in the centre of South Shields: Hodgson, *Borough of South Shields*, pp. 120–1.

144 See note for April 16th 1755.

Elisabeth Carr made oath that she served her last year's service at Sunderland Bridge. s.

20th Removed the said Elisabeth Carr from Southwick to the township of Sunderland Bridge in Elvet parish Durham. ss.

Mary Deans single-woman of Monk Wearmouth swore a bastard to George Lakenby of ditto mariner and I granted general warrant against him. sm.

21st Wrote to John Jeffarson of Harton to pay his servant's wages 6s. o.

[*page* 89] *1760* [*1 stroke*]

February 25th Granted special warrant against Mary Henderson and Mary Baker of Monk Wearmouth spinsters for assaulting at divers times Hugh Riot of ditto mariner with stones and threatening his life. sm.

March 1st Elisabeth Denton of Washington [*inserted,* widow] swore her being with child by William Hunter of Monk Wearmouth keelman and I granted a general warrant against William Hunter. sm.

Signed Sunderland book for a rate 6d.[145]

3rd Granted special warrant against William Archer of Sunderland master and mariner for cruelly beating and bruising his apprentice Stephen Falp. s. Agreed.

5th Granted special warrant against John Parkin, alias Parker of Monk Wearmouth shoemaker for beating and bruising Jane Oswald of ditto widow. sm. Agreed at 14s.

8th Granted special warrant against Edward Wear of Shields saltmaker for defaming and declaring that he had laid with the wife of Sarah the wife of James Reed of ditto, ditto. sm.

---

145 See note for March 23rd 1751.

24th Granted summon<s> warrant against Mr Smithson, Hodgson and Robert Walker for not paying their poor rates. sss. To appear on the 29th. They all agreed to pay.

Removed Mary Deans from Monk Wearmouth to Morton-in-the-Whins in the parish of Dalton le Hole. sss.

Granted special warrant against William Graham of Shields blacksmith for not coming to the servitude of Thomas Richardson of North Shields, as agreed betwixt them. s.

[*page* 90] *1760*

March 29th Granted special warrant against George Crawford of Shields glassman for bruising with an iron shovel Mary Scot widow. sm.

April 2nd Granted general warrant against Michael Rickaby of Whitburn labourer for detaining 16s and 2d from Mary Ellison due to her for labours. *Note* He payed all.

3rd Granted special warrant against Ann wife of John Lyster of Sunderland keelman for bruising Mary Weland wife of Luke of ditto keelman. sm. Agreed.

Took the deposition of Hannah Menham upon oath against her husband Thomas Menham of Shields glassmaker. sm. Agreed by Mr Cookson.

4th Granted special warrant against John Husband and James Mannel of Shields saltmakers for throwing on the fire, putting the little finger out of joynt and greivously bruising Dorothy wife of William Jefferson keelman. sm. Agreed.

N.B. Mary wife of Jacob Callendar of Shields alehouse-keeper, refused to take her oath, though she was by all the time – Remember her husband at the licensing.

7th Granted general warrant against Sarah Yellowly [*inserted*, of Suddick widow] for stopping 15s for wages due to Mary Watson. s *Note* She paid all.

Granted special warrant against John Kell of Shields blacksmith for beating John Rutter of ditto blacksmith. sm. Agreed.

9th Granted summons warrant against [*blank*] Clark miller of Shields for cruelly beating his servant. s. Agreed.

[*page* 91] *1760* [*10 strokes*]

April 11th Granted special warrant against Ann Telfit of Sunderland potseller for bruising with a coal rake Thomas Heaton on his forhead, and threatening his and his wife Elisabeth<'s> life and breaking their windows. sm.

12th Granted summons warrant against James Boag or Bogie of Shields fisherman for calling and declaring that he was able to prove Robert Cousin of ditto, ditto, a thief, and I summoned him to enter into recognizance to make legal proof of the same. sm.

14th Granted general warrant against John Jefferson of Harton farmer for refusing to pay 6s wages to Percival Hall. s.

Granted warrant for distreining the goods of several in the constablery of Monk Wearmouth Shore to George Bryan. ss.

Sent summons warrant to the overseer of the poor of Monk Wearmouth Shore in behalf of Margaret Davison and 3 or 4 children, all small, and her husband John Davison in the King's service. s.

15th Ordered her 1s per week, and each child 6d by Edward Lander who appeared.

[*page* 92] *1760*

21st Granted special warrant against Margaret Anderson of Shields spinster for beating and threatening [*blank*] Rockwood an infant. s.
Agreed.

Granted summons warrant against Margaret Loggan for calling [*blank*] Thompson wife of [*blank*] Thompson of Shields lighterman [*inserted*, a strumpet] and that she could prove her so. s.

April 21st Adjudged the indenture between [*blank*] Hog boat-builder of Shields and [*blank*] Ridley his apprentice to be given up. ss. Ditto and Blagdon.

24th Granted summons warrant against James Dicks of Monk Wearmouth shipwright upon the oath of Thomas Lawson of ditto trimmer that he was drunk on the 23rd. s.

Granted special warrant against Mary wife of John Jefferson of Harton farmer for threatening to burn the corn stacks or do a mischief to the cattle of her son-in-law John Jefferson of the same farmer. sm. Agreed.

28th Wrote to Matthew Ridley Esq. about Elisabeth Richardson and her 3 children's settlement at Heaton. o.[146]

May 1st Granted special warrant against Jane Chamber of Shields spinster for throwing water and beating Mary Ponder and sister. sm. Agreed.

Granted special warrant against Jane Allison wife of George trimmer at the Shoreside, for charging Thomas Hedley of ditto sawyer with stealing an elm slab. sm. [*margin*, Note: She paid all]

2nd Granted special warrant against Mr James Hedley of Scarborough master for cruelly beating and bruising his apprentice William Morriss. s. Agreed.

5th Isable Robinson Spinster of the parish of Monk Wearmouth swore herself to be with child by John Jones of Captain Blomburgh's Company Yorkshire Militia now at Durham.

[*page* 93] *1760* [*5 strokes*]

May 13th Granted special warrant against George Smith of Shields carpenter and blacksmith for declaring that Margaret

---

146 Matthew Ridley of Heaton Hall, MP for Newcastle from 1747 to 1778, and mayor three times (the first when he was only 21): R. Welford, *Men of Mark 'Twixt Tyne and Tweed* (London and Newcastle, 1895), vol. 3, p. 319.

Spraggons widow had inveigled [*blank*] Yarrow and others to steal iron spikes and nails and then to buy them. sm. Agreed.

Granted special warrant against Elisabeth wife of John Story of Monk Weamouth mariner for bruising Jane wife of Ralph Allison of ditto mariner. sm.

Granted special warrant against George Welch [*inserted,* Junior] of Monk Wearmouth keelman for beating and threatening William Howes of ditto, ditto. sm.

15th Granted special warrant against William Graham of South Shields blacksmith for not coming to the service according to his agreement with Thomas Richardson of North Shields blacksmith. s.
Agreed at a guinea from William Graham.

19th Granted special warrant against Mary Marshall widow and Ann her daughter of Bishop Wearmouth for throwing stones and threatening the lifes of Ann Brown and Elisabeth Lawson. sm.

20<th> Granted general warrant against John Stokel of Ryop[147] farmer for detaining £1 from the wages of Catherine Brown of Sunderland widow and milkseller. s.

21st Granted special warrant against George Shanks of Pallion for leaving his master George Langstaff's brick work. o.

22nd Granted special warrant against Paul Killroey of Shields glassmaker for bruising William Anderson of ditto labourer. sm. Agreed.

23rd Granted special warrant against William Matthew of West Boldon tanner for beating William Hedgey. sm.

Made William Matthew's mittimus.

---

147 I.e. Ryhope.

[*page* 94] *1760*

May 23rd Granted general warrant against Thomas Shepherd (late of Byker Hill Northumberland) for leaving the service of John Kirton farmer. s. [*margin,* Dismissed]

24th Granted general warrant against Lancelot Byars of Monk Wearmouth master and mariner for threatening to kill his wife Mary Byars. sm.

26th Granted special warrant against Isabella wife of Thomas Hunter off[148] Monk Wearmouth keelman for calling a whore and threatening the life of Elinor wife of Michael Hunter of ditto keelman. sm. Agreed.

Wrote to Mr Wilkinson Shoreside about [*inserted,* his sons] cruelly using his apprentice Wanless by biting his toes etc. o.

27th Granted special warrant against Thomas Jefferson labourer of Shields for bruising Thomas Crawford [*deleted,* yeoman; *inserted,* glazier]. sm.

[*blank*] against ditto for bruising William Holesby labourer of ditto. sm.

29th Ordered Jane Tate an infant 1s 6d weekly from the overseers of Monk Wearmouth. o.[149]

Granted general warrant against William Lee of Sunderland mariner of the press gang for assaulting and wounding with a cutlass on her thigh Dorothy Olive of Monk Wearmouth. sm.[150]

Granted general warrant against Thomas Emmerson of Sunderland master for cruelly beating John Steel apprentice to Mr William Rafton of Sunderland owner. s.

---

148 I.e. of.

149 Three red pencil strokes in left margin.

150 Three red pencil strokes in left margin.

[*page* 95] *1760*

May 31st Removed Mary Henderson of Monk Wearmouth widow to East Renton in Houghton-le-Spring parish. ss.

Removed [*blank*] widow from Whitburn to Hely or Heleigh in North Witton chapelry in Hartburn. sss.

June 2nd Sworn in Gilbert Purviss shoemaker for constable of East Pans Ward in Shields, as I did the workhouse master [*inserted*, Graham] for Middle Pans. s.

Granted special warrant against John Swan of Shields glass-blower for beating and bruising William Catcherside of the 31st May. sm.
Agreed, each paying half charges.

Granted general warrant upon oath of Mr John Scurfield overseer of Great Usworth against Martha Stoddard for threatening to leave her 3 children upon the parish. sm.

Committed Martha Stoddard to the House of Correction for a month. s. Superseded.

5th Granted special warrant against William Gent of Monk Wear-mouth keelman for beating Mr William Tewart of the same. sm.

Summoned overseer of Monk Wearmouth to show cause why Mary Baker and child should not be relieved. s.

Granted special warrant against Jane Twist of Sunderland ale-seller and widow for hiring certain persons and coming with them to break open the doors of Jane Hunter of ditto aleseller, (and I fear a bad woman). sm.[151]

6th Granted special warrant against Joseph Dryden of Carrs Hill

151 Entry crossed through in black pencil; two blue pencil strokes in left margin; two red pencil strokes in right margin; 'aleseller, (and I fear a bad woman)' underlined in blue pencil.

in Jarro gin-wright for defrauding Joseph Haddon of ditto tallow chandler of a peruka and assaulting him. sm. Agreed.

[*page* 96] *1760*

June 6th Granted special warrant against [*blank*] of Sunderland alekeeper for beating and wounding near the eye [*deleted,* Debora Hartley; *inserted* Deborah Arkley]. sm.
[*margin,* Note] Deborah Arkley is a very bad woman. Agreed at 3s 6d.

Committed William Gent of Monk Wearmouth to goal for want of sureties. ss.

7th Committed Jane Twist of Sunderland aleseller and widow to gaol for want of sureties. o.

9th Took sureties of William Gent in £20 and Richard Broom in<n>holder in £10 and William Telford keelman in £10, all of Monk Wearmouth. sssm.

Granted general warrant against Robert Storey and Mary Johnson late of Priestwick in Ponteland parish for leaving the service of John Forster of East Boldon farmer. s. N.B. They returned.

10th Granted special warrant against Robert Sevil of Bishop Wearmouth baker for bruising Jane Moffat his servant and turning her away. [*margin,* N.B. He paid a quarter's wages and expenses]

Took sureties of widow Jane Twist in £20, and Mr George Thompson [*inserted,* fitter of Sunderland] in £20, for her appearance at sessions. sss.[152]

11th Granted special warrant against Mary wife of Robert Younghusband of Shields keelman for wounding both Isable Green and Mary Horn of ditto upon their heads. sm. Agreed.

---

152 There is no record of Jane Twist's appearance at the quarter sessions.

12th Granted general warrant against William Morris apprentice for leaving the service of James Hedley of Scarborough master and mariner. s. Agreed.

[*page* 97] *1760*

June 13th Granted special warrant against Mary wife of James Laidler labourer of Berkley Fell for assaulting and threatening the life of Jane wife of George Dixon of ditto waggoner. sm.

18th Granted special warrant against John Dodds of Bent House near Shields, servant, for bruising Mary Richardson of ditto. sm. [*inserted, Dismissed*]
[*margin,* N.B.] Mary Richardson is a sorry girl.

25th Summoned overseer of Washington upon account of Jane Carre widow aged 43.

26th Granted special warrant to the constable of Whitburn to seize the goods of Martha Rawling widow, which she lately within 5 days conveyed out of the house of George Dixon farmer, in order to defraud him of *rents*.

30th Granted special warrant against Elisabeth Turner of Bishop Wearmouth for beating and bruising Thomasine Plains of Numbers Garth. sm. Agreed, a like warrant being granted by Mr Hutton.[153]

Granted special warrant against John Cough the Elder and John Cough the Younger of Shields salters, for beating and bruising James Mannel, and Elisabeth his wife. sm.

July 2nd Granted special warrant against William Wood of Shields glassman for bruising and cutting Hannah wife of Stephen Peacock. sm.

---

153 Robert Hutton, an active magistrate; though of Houghton-le-Spring, he and Teasdale Mowbray tended to act together in Sunderland for settlement examinations and other routine business: DRO, Q/S/OB 11, pp. 150, 206–7; Q/S/OB 12, p. 114.

Took oath of widow [*blank*] Scot adm<inistrato>r to her husband, late of the ship Lizard in his Majesty's service and not worth £20. o.

[*page* 98] *1760*

July 5th William Tewart released William Gent, and Jane Hunter released Jane Twist from their respective recognizances. o.o.

7th Granted special warrant against Ralph Hall of Whitburn farmer for bruising Elisabeth wife of Joseph Dodds farmer. sm. *Agreed at 5s and charges*, or to find security.

Granted general warrant against Charles MacKenzye master of the ship called the Fells now at Shields, for not paying £12 wages to Thomas Conway, mariner, a poor Irishman. o.

8th Granted general warrant against [*blank*] Ramshaw and John Craik for leaving the service of Mrs Jennison and partners. s.[154]

11th Granted special warrant against William Gibson, [*blank*] Purvis etc. for defrauding William Middleyard and 2 others all of Shields coblemen of £2 10s 0d wages. s. Agreed at 12s 6d.

14th Discharged William son of William Smith of Sunderland from his apprenticeship to Francis Wilson of Whitby master and mariner, the said Wilson's ship being seized, he in prison, and not paid the annual wages to William Smith. ss.

18th Granted special warrant against Elisabeth Bulmer of Monk Wearmouth wife of George Bulmer keelman for charging William Chambers of Monk Wearmouth with having a false key and opening the barn of Mr James Smithson of ditto. s.

---

154 Mrs Jennison and Partners who had a mine on Pelton Common (near Chester-le-Street), during the disturbances in 1765 advertised in the press pointing out that the arson committed there was a capital offence, without benefit of clergy: *Newcastle Courant* 4644, 21 September 1765.

[*page* 99] *1760*

July 22nd Granted general warrant against William Archer of Sunderland master and mariner for detaining £1 19s 6d the wages of Robert Hacksly deceased from his father Robert a blind man. o.

Granted general warrant against Anthony Cousins of Shields keelman for getting with child Jane Rogers single woman of ditto who swore it to him. sm.

Removed Sarah Precise widow and 3 children from Shields to Monk Wearmouth Shoreside. sss.

23rd Removed Edward Donkin son of Edward now a mariner in his Majesties service from Hylton Lordship to Monk Wearmouth Shoreside. sss.

24<th> Granted special warrant against Elisabeth Barford of Shields singlewoman for beating and wounding upon the eye Ann Shields of ditto ditto. sm.
Agreed at 8s and 6d, but the girl ran away.

Granted special warrant against Hugh Cow or Cough salter for bruising William Commin of Shields agent. sm.

26th Took the information of William Commin against Dorothy wife of Hugh Cow for 8 profane oaths and curses. 1s.[155]

Committed Hugh Cow to the House of Correction for want of sureties. ss.[156]

Wrote to Mr Thomas Dixon about the complaint of ten apprentices for wages due in their absence in Christmass Holy-days, and adjudged the complaint unreasonable. o.

155 Three blue pencil strokes in left margin; 'profane oaths' underlined in blue pencil.

156 Three blue pencil strokes in left margin; 'House of Correction' underlined in blue pencil.

[*page* 100] *1760*

July 28th Made Ralph Hall's (of Whitburn farmer) mittimus to gaol, he having farther threatened to cut out the puddings etc. ss. [*margin*, Superseded]

29th Granted general warrant against Thomas Pringle blacksmith for deserting the service of widow Wheatley of Monk Wearmouth. s. Acquitted, having been heard before Mr Mowbray.[157]

30th Made Dorothy Cow alias Cough's mittimus to gaol for swearing and cursing 8 times. ss.
[*margin*, Note: She paid 8s and 1s charges]

August 4th Granted special warrant against George Partis of Monk Wearmouth labourer for assaulting Alexander Mills of ditto stonecutter. sm.

Granted special warrant against Sarah Armstrong widow, and Jane Henderson of the Pans Bishop Wearmouth for assaulting and cutting Leonard Carre of ditto labourer on the forhead. sm. Agreed at <£1 15s 0d>. They are all bad people.

5th Granted special warrant against Mary Richardson of Shields spinster for assaulting and threatening the life of John Dodds her fellow servant. sm.
[*margin*, Agreed]

8th Granted general warrant against Samuel Haw, Peter Atkins and Timothy Stewart of Great Yarmouth masters for beating the boatman of [*blank*] Coxon and taking away the little wherry boat from her moorings on the 7th instant. sm.

Ordered the overseers of Monk Wearmouth to pay Mary Bell and 4 small children 12s per month. o.

---

157 See earlier note, p. 125: Teasdale Mowbray, a magistrate active on the bench in Sunderland and Bishopwearmouth; for example DRO, Q/S/OB 12, p.114.

Ordered ditto to pay 8s per month to Elisabeth Coxon and 2 infants. o.

[*page* 101] *1760*

August 9th Granted special warrant against William Catton of Sunderland master, for harbouring William Tinsel a soldier in Lord Charles Manners Regiment. o. [*margin*, Agreed for 2 guineas with Captain Perring]

11th Granted special warrant against Matthew Cook of Sunderland Pans boatman [*inserted*, and constable] for assaulting Leonard Carre [*inserted*, of ditto labourer] and defrauding him of £1 15s 0d. sm. Agreed and paid all, and there is not a greater villain than Cook.

12th Granted general warrant against Robert Lawrence of Bishop Wearmouth master for detaining the wages £2. 10s. 0d due to his apprentice Robert Harle. s.

13th Wrote to Edward Maxwell of Whitburn about detaining his maid's wages. o.

18th Granted general warrant against Andrew Hedley and 5 more apprentices to William Todd of the Shore ship-builder for refusing to work, except at tyde hours. s. Bound all over on the 19th in £10 penalty.

19th Granted special warrant against William Taylor of the press-gang Shields for beating Ann Hall and her mother Elisabeth Park both of Shields. sm.

23rd Granted special warrant against Thomas Dixon of Sunderland Pans master and mariner for beating and violently throwing into the hold against the coals Edward Tinmouth of Monk Wearmouth keelman. sm.

26<th> Granted general warrant against Elisabeth Killock wife of James of Shields shoemaker, Mary Ogle of the same spinster having sworn the peace against her. sm.

[*page* 102] *1760* [*1 stroke*]

August 27th Summoned Isable Reed of Shields fruiterer to show cause why she should not be punished for drunkenness on the 25th and 26th instant upon the information on the oath of Mary Reed of ditto widow. o.

Granted special warrant against the said Isable Reed, Jane Pye of ditto widow having sworn the peace against her. o.

30th Granted [*deleted*, general; *inserted*, special] warrant against John Longstaff of Bishop Wearmouth ship-carpenter to prove his charge of Jane wife of Robert Anderson mason stealing deals. sm.

September 1st Granted general warrant against Thomas Atkinson of Monk Wearmouth mate for defrauding Benjamin Thompson of 2 guineas. s. [*margin*, Dismissed]

Granted general warrant against 3 boys servants on board the Viper (Mr James Smithson's ship) viz. Luke Carr, John Berry, and Robert the Londoner, for breaking open a chest and feloniously carrying away £2 2s 0d the property of Benjamin Thompson from the said chest the property of Thomas Atkinson mate of the said Viper. s.

3rd Granted general warrant against John Edwards shipwright of the Shore for beating and t<e>aring the shirt of Thomas Arnot of ditto. sm.

9th Granted general warrant against Joshua Joplin of Westo servant man for refusing to obey the lawfull commands of his master William Burn of the Lay-gate. ss.

Granted general warrant against Margaret Dodds wife of Jo: Dodds of Whitburn for beating her maid and encouraging her to steal coals and pease from her neighbors. o.

[*page* 103] *1760* [*2 strokes*]

September 12th Granted general warrant against Richard Parker and wife for lying in wait 4 hours, and threatening to have the blood of Richard Graham, all keelmen of Under Offerton. sm.

17th Granted general warrant against George Wake (late of Berwick) and now of Sunderland master and mariner for not maintaining his bastard male child born 6th April of the body of Ann Norton. sm.

20th Granted general warrant against Jane wife of James Moore of Shields keelman for charging John Rutter blacksmith with stealing iron from Mrs Blagdon and selling it to Ann Bone of ditto widow. sm.

22nd Granted general warrant against John Potts of the Shoreside shipwright upon the oath of Isable Robinson of Fulwell to find security for the child she is pregnant with. sm. s.

Granted general warrant against Jane Nesbit wife of James labourer of Shields for declaring George Turner to have the venereal disease and thereby preventing his selling his butter and milk. s.

October 10th Committed John Potts to gaol for want of security. ss.

Granted general warrant against James Kirk of the Shoreside shopkeeper for detaining 11s 8½d from his hired servant Ann Lyster. s. He paid all.

[*page* 104] *1760*

October 15th Granted general warrant against Robert Rutter of Shields saltmaker for beating Bartholomew Musgrave chapel-warden in the execution of his office whilst he was inspecting the alehouses last *Sunday morning*. sm.

November 4th Granted general warrant against Robert Thompson of the parish of Easington farmer for detaining £1 2s 9d wages of Ann Hall. o.

Granted special warrant against William Catcherside apprentice to Mr Evan Deere for refusing to obey his master's orders. o. [*margin*, Mem. I sent him to the Regulating Captain][158]

15th Granted general warrant against Edward Smelt of Shoreside mason for detaining 12s from John Spence and William Woolston of ditto labourers. s.

17th Granted special warrant against Nicholas Storey barber of the Shoreside for throwing a full tankard of ale and a candlestick in the face of John Shute joiner. o.[159]

Wrote to Mr Todd ship builder about the usage of his apprentice John Laidler. o.

Removed Isable Robinson from Fulwell to Alnwick in Northumberland. ss.

Committed John Potts to the House of Correction who hath got her with child. ss.

21st Granted special warrant against Fidlerr Gasket and Hugh Cow trimmers for detaining 2s 9d wages from James Pyle trimmer all of Shields. s.

[*page* 105] *1760*

November 22nd Granted special warrant against Robert Thwait steward to Mr Fairless saltpans, and Hugh Cow labourer for cruelly beating and bruising Elinor Hall spinster of Shields. sm. [*margin*, Note: They paid £1 1s 0d and all charges]

24<th> Granted special warrant against Michael Robson and Samuel Wilson of Sunderland shoemakers, for bruising John Sparks of ditto shoemaker and Margaret his wife. sm.

25th Granted general warrant against John Dawson of Shields

158 The Regulating Captain managed the local press gang on the rivers, usually storing the 'recruits' on a tender at the mouth of the Tyne.

159 Entry crossed through in black pencil; three blue pencil strokes in left margin.

mason for detaining <£>2 1<s> 0<d> from the wages of Alexander Gregg labourer. s.

26<th> Granted special warrant against Jacob Wilsons of Bill-key apprentice <to> John Fenwick for refusing to obey his master. ss.

27th Granted general warrant against [*blank*] Skipsey of Lay-gate Shields[160] for not paying 18s 2d to Ann Hedley for wages. o. Dismissed and the girl is a bad girl.

27th I took the information and granted a peace warrant against Thomas Menham of Shields glassmaker, upon the oath of his wife Hannah. ssss.

28th Granted general warrant against Thomas Marshall of Hebburn farmer for refusing to pay the wages of Ann Arnot his servant. s.

December 1st Sent a liberate to the House of Correction for John Potts. s.

6th Granted special warrant against John Buck of Sunderland mason for defrauding Thomas Vary of Shields junior of above £2. <5>s. 0d. s.

[*page* 106] *1760*

December 8th Granted general warrant against John Thompson of Shields maltmaker, for threatening the life of Henry Gibson of ditto boatman. sm.

11th Granted special warrant against James Cay of Heworth quarryman for turning of<f> Richard Brown labourer before his time. s.

22nd Granted general warrant against David Stobbs ballast heaver of Shields for bruising Robert Alexander of ditto labourer. sm.

---

160 Around 'Lay-gate Shields' the text is crossed through in black pencil.

Summons to the overseer of L<ow> Heworth. s.

29th Granted special warrant against Joseph Miles and Elinor his wife, and Ann Hall wife of Miles Hall mariner, all of Shields, for beating and threatening Margaret Fawcett and Matthew her son. sm. Agreed at 8s. 6d.

30th Granted general warrant against Thomas Davison of Bishop Wearmouth skipper upon the oath of Dorothy Marley of Barmston [*inserted,* about a fortnight after Lammas] that she is with child by him. ssss.

[*page* 107] *1761* [*5 strokes*]

January 1st Granted special warrant against Joseph Pearson of Lambton pitman for feloniously stealing and carrying away a cock chicken, the property of George Walker of South Biddick. sm.

6th Granted special warrant against Thomas Potts servant to Mr Stafford of Monk Wearmouth Shore for bruising James Atkinson of ditto on the 23rd December, who hath been under a surgeon's care ever since. sm.
Agreed.

10th Granted general warrant against John Walker of Shields baker for refusing to pay £3 wages to his servant Jacob Schroder. s.

13th Granted special warrant against Henry Coats of Shields fisherman for bruising and inhumanly beating his wife Jane. sm.

17<th> Granted general warrant against Joseph Greenwell late butcher, and William Hunter labourer of Fulwell for abusing and threatening the life of Edward Brass of ditto labourer. sm. Agreed.

Granted special warrant against Margaret, wife of Gawen Stotle of Monk Wearmouth skipper for charging Ann Langdon of ditto with stealing a skeel from Mr James Smithson. s.

21st Granted general warrant against George Hedley of Chester farmer for detaining £2 9s 0d wages from William Clark. s. Agreed.

30th Removed Elisabeth Beadland widow, Ann and James both infants, from Usworth to Birtley. ss.

Granted special warrant against J. Davidson and 3 other apprentices to William Tewart of Monk Wearmouth for deserting his service. s. Agreed.

[*page* 108] *1761*

February 6th Granted special warrant against Robert Brown of Monk Wearmouth trimmer for assaulting and wounding in the face Alexander Robertson of Sunderland schoolmaster. sm. Agreed.

7th Granted special warrant against George Lockey of Sunderland joiner for charging Archibald Purviss of Monk Wearmouth innholder with theft. sm.

9th Granted special warrant against Andrew Gregg taylor and Mary his wife of Monk Wearmouth for cruelly burning and striking with a poker their apprentice William Taylor. s. Parted.[161]

11th Granted general warrant against Robert Curry and [*blank*] Horn of Pelton for leaving the service of Robert Turner of Sunderland master and mariner to whom they are apprentices. s. Agreed.

18th Granted special warrant against Aaron Gaskarth of Shields ballast-heaver for assaulting and t<e>aring of the cloak of Mary Welton, alias Blair, and a summons to Sarah Story to appear. sm. Agreed.

19th Granted general warrant against John Kell of Shields mariner for [*inserted*, attempting and] threatening mischief to William Crosby and Elisabeth his wife. ss.

---

161 Entry crossed through in black pencil; two blue pencil strokes in left margin.

20th Sent order to the overseers of Hylton to provide for Jane and Elisabeth Wilson.

23rd Granted general warrant against William Gent servant to William How of Monk Wearmouth for deserting his service. s. Agreed.

[*page* 109] *1761* [*5 strokes*]

March 9th Granted special warrant against James Gilderoy and James Mow of Bell Key glassman [*sic*] for assaulting etc. Richard Fawel chapel warden of Heworth for rebuking them, for swearing. s.m. Agreed.

Granted general warrant against Robert Cousins of Shields wright for beating and cutting the chin of James Bogie of ditto maltman. sm.

13th Granted general warrant against Edward Storer of Shields bricklayer for beating and knocking out a tooth of John Henzell glassmaker of ditto on the 12th instant. sm. Run of<f>.

18th Granted special warrant against David Allen for beating and abusing Archibald Boey wherryman, both of Shields. sm.

19th Granted special warrant against Robert Crisp of Jarrow Wood farmer upon his wife's Margaret swearing the peace against him. sm.
Agreed betwixt them.

27<th> Granted special warrant against Ann wife of Thomas Clark of Shields glassman for charging Jane Scot widow with feloniously detaining her linnen shift. (Not served).

28th Granted special warrant against John Watson [*inserted,* junior] of Shields butcher for assaulting and bruising John Jackson apprentice to Edward Davison of ditto boatbuilder. sm. Dismissed.

30th Granted general warrant against Thomas Carter for leaving his master Alexander Morton's service before the expiration of his apprenticeship, both of Monk Wearmouth Shore. s. Agreed.

[*page* 110] *1761*

April 6th Granted general warrant against Thomas Brown of Sunderland mariner for breaking open the cabbin door and chest of John Colson master and mariner and feloniously stealing £4 or £5 in English and Holland money, the property of the said John Colson out of his ship called the Providence on the 3rd instant. sm.

13th Granted special warrant against Thomas Richardson of Shields blacksmith for assaulting and bruising William Forsyth taylor of ditto. sm.
Agreed.

14th Granted special warrant against Robert Turner of Hebburn joyner for charging [*blank*] Mayors of Jarro-Key blacksmith with false weights to buy and sell by. sm.
Agreed.

Granted summons warrant against several persons at Monk Wearmouth Shore for refusing to pay their poor rates to appear at the quarter sessions upon complaint of Samuel Stephenson overseer. s.

15th Granted general warrant against Thomas Croskat of Monk Wearmouth Shore carpenter for getting Mary Hall with child, upon the oath of the said Mary. ssm. Agreed to marry.

16th Granted general warrant against William Pye mariner of Monk Wearmouth for getting with child Jane Dobson of ditto servant to Edward Browel master, upon the oath of the said Jane. ssss.

20th Granted general warrant against Henry Dixon apprentice to George Hopper of Sunderland [*deleted*, master mariner; *inserted*, boat builder] for deserting his service. s.
Returned him to his service.

23rd Removed Katherine Thompson an ideot from Low Heworth to All Saints, Newcastle. sss.[162]

[*page* 111] *1761* [*5 strokes*]

April 23rd Bound over George Robinson master and mariner of Monk Wearmouth to answer the complaint of John Graham for wages at Shore, under the penalty of £20, or to pay £1. Superseded.

Granted general warrant against William Reed of Monk Wearmouth ship carpenter for getting Margaret Nicholson with child, upon the oath of the said Margaret. sss. Deferred.

27th Granted special warrant against William Forsyth of Shields taylor for breaking open the door of Isable Richardson and threatening her life. sm.Agreed at 5s.

Granted special warrant against William Forster of Shields cobleman for threatening the life of Catherine Tinmouth wife of John, and charging her with adultery. sm.
Agreed.

Granted special warrant against Thomas Dixon [*inserted,* junior] of Monk Wearmouth shipwright for defrauding John Porter constable of a warrant against his apprentice William Reed. s. Deferred.

Granted special warrant against Jane and Isable Lumsdale of Bishop Wearmouth spinsters for assaulting beating and breaking the windows of Elisabeth Turner. sm.
Dismissed.

May 5th Granted warrant against William Matthew of West Boldon for assaulting with an [*inserted,* prong] fork and threatening to run it into the body of Alice Gelston, and carrying away her room door etc. o.

---

162 See note 68 at April 16th 1755.

Committed the said William Matthew to Durham Goal, till he find sureties. o.

Granted special warrant against John Addison's maid Elisabeth [*blank*] for defrauding the old fool of cloaths, ring and money. o.

[*page* 112] 1761

May 9th Granted general warrant against Isable Weer of Shields spinster for feloniously stealing, carrying away and offering to sale a peice of lead, value 1s 10d, the property of Messrs Cookson and Co. sm.

Granted special warrant against John Robinson of Monk Wearmouth hatter for assaulting and throwing stones etc. into the dwelling chamber of Elinor and Ann Dicks. sm. [*margin*, Agreed.]

Committed the above Isable Wear to goal. s.

12th Granted general warrant against Mary the wife of [*blank*] Wood of Southwick labourer upon suspicion of her stealing <£> 1 10<s> 0<d> from Elisabeth Andrews of ditto aged 80. o. Fo<r> Mr Gray.

13th Granted special warrant against Ann Harrison of Monk Wearmouth for refusing to come to her service as hired by Mr J. Edwards of ditto ship builder. s.
Mem She came to live with J. Edwards.

Granted special warrant against Jacob Speed of Birtley pitman for not paying 9s 10d to Catherine Snowden widow for wages. o.

14th Granted general warrant against Hannah Peacock of Shields for assaulting with a peice of iron Elisabeth wife of John Bridekirk of East Row near Whitby. sm.

Granted special warrant against John Rogerson of Sunderland for refusing to come to the service of Andrew Brown of Monk Wearmouth miller. s
Note He went to his place, and paid charges.

15th Committed Mary Peacock to Durham Goal for want of sureties. ss.

[*page* 113] *1761*

May 18th Granted general warrant against George Man of Hylton Lordship for beating Thomas Potts of H<igh> Bridge. sm.

June 20th Granted general warrant against John Brown of East Boldon carpenter for assaulting and threatening Robert Matthew etc. sm.

Took the information of Barbare Matthew of ditto against the said John Brown for swearing 5 oaths. s.[163]

Convicted the said John Brown upon the above information of his confession and he paid 5s (and charges 2) which were given to the poor of Boldon by the constable William Harbottle.[164]

22nd Took the information of William Nevins of Whitburn plowman against John Browel waller and William French weaver for prophanely cursing him at Whitburn on the 21st. s.[165]

23<rd> Took the deposition of Mary Rutter of Shields, that she is now with child and that Edward Sarson an Invalid is the father. s.

23rd Granted general warrant against Edward Sarson aforesaid on complaint of the overseer of Shields. sm.

25th Granted special warrant against George Hedley of Harraton Outside for refusing to pay the wages £3 13s 0d due to William and Catherine Clark. s.

Granted special warrant against Robert Commin of Shields blockmaker for bruising Ann wife of Grantham Harper. sm.

---

163 Entry crossed through in black pencil.
164 Entry crossed through in black pencil.
165 Entry crossed through in black pencil; 'prophanely cursing him' underlined in blue pencil.

[*page* 114] *1761*

June 26th Granted general warrant against James Deare [*inserted*, Captain] Lieutenant of the Invalids for getting Elisabeth Adey with child upon the oath of the said Elisabeth a month before Candlemass last. ssss.

27th Granted special warrant against Jane the wife of Peter Cooper blacksmith of the Shoreside for beating bruising and threatening Elinor wife of William Hastings of ditto mason. sm.

29th Committed Robert Commin of Shields blockmaker to gaol for want of sureties, and for impudence to myself. ss. Superseded.

Granted general warrant against Mary Moore and Ann Sanderson of Shields saltmakers for deserting the service of John Lynsch of ditto saltmaker. s.

Granted special warrant against Ann Younghusband, wife of James of Shields shoemender for throwing a calf's foot at, and threatening the life of, Mary Jacobs of ditto widow. sm.

July 1st Committed Ann Husband to the House of Correction.

Ordered overseer of Monk Wearmouth to receive Christiana Watson and infant into their workhouse. o.

2nd Granted general warrant against Elisabeth Chicken for leaving the service of Robert Bowery of Hauxley Hill farmer and carrying away £2 2s 11½d with her. s.

19th Removed Christian Watson [*inserted*, and Robert] an infant son of Robert and Christian Watson cooper of Morpeth, in Northumberland to ditto from the township of Monk Wearmouth. sss.

Removed John Robson hatter from Monk Wearmouth Shore to Gateshead. sss.

[*page* 115] *1761*

July 14th Granted special warrant against [*blank*] wife of William Varey of Shields mariner for beating Lewis Ogle, when collecting the window tax. sm.

17th Granted special warrant against Ann Robson of Birtley widow for threatening the life of Jane Catel midwife of ditto. sm.

30th Ordered overseer of Jarro to pay Ann Anderson widow her arrears of 9d per week. o.

August 1st Granted special warrant against Elisabeth Hall wife of Matthew Hall of Monk Wearmouth labourer for beating Jane wife of John Allen of ditto labourer. sm.

3rd Granted general warrant against Ann and Alice Watson of Whitburn for beating and bruising Jane and William Purviss of ditto. sm.

Thomasine Hood of Shields spinster swore herself to be with child by Thomas Wilson of ditto shoemaker. s.

4th Granted general warrant against Thomas Menham of Shields glassmaker upon his wife Hannah's swearing the peace against him for bruising her head and arm with an iron poker. sm.

Granted general warrant against John Anderson of Monk Wearmouth mariner for assaulting with a pistol and drawn sword John Brown of Sunderland merchant. sm.

Granted general warrant against Thomas Wilson of Shields aforementioned for securing the township upon the oath of Thomasine Hood aforesaid. sm.

[*page* 116] *1761*

August 8th Took the recognizance of John Anderson of Monk Wearmouth mariner [*inserted,* in £40], John Hudson of ditto barber in £20, and Francis Fetherstonehalgh weaver of Elvet in

Durham in £20, for the personal appearance of the said John Anderson at the next general quarter sessions for Durham. sm.[166]

10th Granted general warrant against Margaret wife of Richard Holmes of Monk Wearmouth labourer for threatening the lifes of Margaret and Margaret Purviss of ditto mother and daughter. sm.
Agreed at 5s for expenses.

Granted special warrant against Elisabeth widow, Elisabeth, Thomas and Joseph Pearson all of High Lambton, for assaulting and bruising Mary wife of Cuthbert Holt of ditto pitman and threatening her life. sm.

13th Granted general warrant against Thomas Fairgreave or Greave of Monk Wearmouth glazier for assaulting and bruising Margaret Roxby of ditto with an iron poker on her head and hand, and for beating and kicking her two daughters Margaret and Elisabeth. sm. Agreed.

17th Granted search warrant against Isable Heath's house of Shields widow at the sign of the Sugar Loaf upon William Chapman seeing [*inserted,* his] great watch coat lately stolen from him in her house. s. Note: she delivered up the coat and paid charges.

Granted general warrant against John Heaton of Monk Wearmouth skipper for refusing to work, though an yearly servant with Mr George Longstaff. o.

[*page* 117] *1761*

August 18th Granted special warrant against Arthur Bell of Cleadon labourer for refusing to pay 10s wages to Mary Jefferson. s. *Note* he proved the contrary and Mary Jefferson's mother paid the expenses.

21st Granted general warrant against George Walsh of Monk Wearmouth skipper for beating and laming the leg of Jacob Pennyman of ditto. sm.

---

166 There is no record of his appearance at the quarter sessions.

22nd Ordered Mary widow of Anthony Thompson mariner to be received with 3 small children into the workhouse of Monk Wearmouth. o.

25<th> Granted peace warrant against Thomas Thornton of Great Yarmouth master upon the oath of John Stafford of Monk Wearmouth farmer. sm.

Took the oath of Elisabeth Potts singlewoman that she is with child by Thomas Blair of Shields mariner and granted a warrant against him. sss.

Granted warrant against Robert Shotton [*inserted,* of Shields tydesman] for beating John Blacklin of Shields glazier. sm.

31<st> Granted general warrant against Margaret wife of Clement Watson of Gateshead labourer for [*inserted,* bruising] the face and breaking the rib of Ann Storey of ditto widow on the 24th. sm.

Granted general warrant against Edward Roseby or Roxby [*inserted,* of Birtley waggon man] for bruising Thomas Potts of Birtley waggon man on the face. sm.

December 21st Granted summons warrant against Elisabeth Wilson and 9 more for stealing pan-coals from Mr Thompson's Key. s.

24<th> Granted general warrant against Elisabeth wife of James Farthing of Sheilds boatman for endeavouring to raise a mob against James Purviss pilot, and to strike him. sm.
Agreed, Elisabeth Farthing paying expenses.

[*page* 118] *1761 & 1762*

December 29th Granted general warrant against John Wood of Southwick limeburner for defrauding John Plumpton of East Boldon of his share of £10 18s 4d paid from Mr J. Gally. s.

29th Distributed Mr Steph<enson>'s bequest of 40s to the 8 following widows:[167]

Barbara Plumpton at 5s
Ann Plumpton
Jane Nichols
Barbara Wood
Widow Wallace
Rebecca Watson
Susan Johnson
Mary Hall

1762

January 24th Sent order to the overseer of Burdon to appear upon complaint of Catherine [*blank*] of Whitburn. o.

26th Rachel Scot of Shields single woman swore her self to be with child by William Lambert of ditto mariner and a warrant was given against him. ssss.

27th Granted general warrant against Catherine Aysbit [*inserted*, of Chorden Fell widow] for defrauding widow Minnakin of High Heworth of a boll of wheat 9s and a goose 1s 8d, part of her agreement for selling her milk. sm. Agreed.

28th Ann Carter of L<ow> Heworth Fell singlewoman swore a bastard to Thomas Mangham of Chester-le-Street carrier, and a warrant was given against him. ssss.

30th Granted special warrant against Christopher Dixon apprentice to Mr Evan Deer of Shields for leaving his work etc. Committed him. sss. Agreed.[168]

February 3rd Granted special warrant against Mary Hunter of Hedworth for [*inserted*, falsely] charging Matthew Hall farmer of Kibblesworth with getting her with child etc. sm.

---

167 In 1759 John Stephenson Esq. of Newcastle left the rents from properties in Westgate to provide 5s 0d each to eight poor widows of Boldon (as well as to others in Aldstone and Garrygill in Cumberland): Surtees, *History and Antiquities*, vol. 2, p. 65.

168 Cookson and Deer owned four saltpans in 1760: Hodgson, *Borough of South Shields*, p. 116.

[*page* 119] *1762* [*5 strokes*]

February 6th Granted general warrant against William Wilson of Heworth Chapelry collier for picking the pocket of John Williamson of ditto collier of 4s. sm. *They agreed.*

8th Convicted Edward Pearson of the Shoreside butcher of drunkenness upon the oath of one credible witness, and he accordingly paid 5s to the poor of the parish of Monk Wearmouth. s.

23rd Elisabeth Ramsay of Shields single woman swore herself to be with child by Richard Forest of ditto carpenter and a warrant was issued against him. ssss.

March 2nd Granted general warrant against Stephen Wilkinson of Sunderland shoemaker for beating cruelly William Allen his apprentice. o.

6th Granted general warrant against Jane Cousins wife of [*inserted,* Anthony] Cousins of Shields boatman for bruising and cutting the nose of Robert Younghusband of ditto boatman. sm. Agreed at 6s.

11th Committed Jane Cousins to goal for want of sureties. Superseded.

15th Granted general warrant against Andrew Lightfoot of Shields shoemaker for beating and threatening Thomas Robinson of ditto shoemaker.

18th Granted general warrant against Robert Crisp of Jarrow Wood farmer for refusing a maintenance to Margaret his wife and turning her out of doors and putting her in fear of life. o.

22nd Granted general warrant against Lancelot Rawling for deserting the service of Mr James Smithson of Monk Wearmouth. s. Agreed.

[*page* 120] *1762* [*4 strokes*]

March 26th Granted general warrant against William Gibson of Shields butcher for threatening the life of Edward Davis of North Shields watchmaker. sm.

27th Granted general warrant against George Pattison late of Plausworth for leaving the service of J. Hill of Westo. s. Not found.

29th Alice Pennyman of Shields singlewoman swore herself with child by Thomas Atkinson of Cleadon ship carpenter. s.

30th Took the recognizance of William Gibson of Shields butcher in £30, and Robert Elliott [*inserted*, shoemaker] and Edward Elder of ditto boat builder in £10 each for William Gibson's appearance at the next quarter sessions. sssm.[169]

April 5th Granted general warrant against Ralph Watson for deserting the service of Thomas Carr of Shields butcher. s.

Granted general warrant against Dorothy wife of Francis Woodnutt of Shields weaver to prosecute Joseph Grant labourer for stealing a wide-cloth coat. s. *Note* The wife of George Nelson of Shields the accuser is a bad (or mad) woman and Joseph Grant intirely innocent.[170]

6th Granted general warrant against James Dicks of the Shoreside carpenter for assaulting and beating Andrew Brown of ditto miller. sm. Agreed.[171]

Wrote to Bowrey, farmer of Harton Down hill to pay wages to his servant, who was got into the Infirmary. o. He paid 6s to him.[172]

---

169 There is no record of his appearance at the quarter sessions.

170 Entry crossed through in black pencil; two blue pencil strokes in left margin.

171 Entry crossed through in black pencil; one blue pencil stroke in left margin.

172 Tew was a governor of Newcastle Infirmary which opened in 1751: see 'Introduction', pp. 3–4.

12th Granted special warrant against William son of William Dobson for beating and bruising his father and taking away an iron pot from him. sm. Made his mittimus. ss. Agreed.

[*page* 121] *1762*

April 12th Granted general warrant against Thomas Dixon of Shields labourer for leaving the service of James Smith of ditto brickmaker. s.
Agreed.

Margaret wife of Robert Crisp of Jarro Wood farmer swore the peace against him and I granted <a> warrant against him. sm.

13th *Mem* Convicted John Donkin of Bell Key, and Robert Collingwood of the Fell Gate (both in the parish of Jarro) in the penalty of 20s each for selling ale without license and I pay'd the said money (according to the 3rd of Charles 1st) into the hands of the churchwardens of Jarro and Heworth, 7s. Returned to the quarter sessions and also the conviction of Ralph Clark below mentioned.[173]

14th Transferred the licence of Lancelot Fenwick of Bell Key to John Donkin, it having been certifyed, that he is of good fame and of sober life and conversation. sm.[174]

15th Granted general warrant against Catherine wife of John Lakeland of Shields bottlemaker for assaulting Joanne Betson with a brick and bruising her. sm. Agreed.

15th Parted Ralph Watson from his master Thomas Carr Butcher of Shields upon the said Thomas receiving eight pounds from the said Ralph Watson. ss.

16<th> Convicted Ralph Clark of Monkton upon his own confession of selling 2 barrels of ale to the above Robert Collingwood and he paid 13s 4d to the poor of Jarro. o.

---

173 Entry crossed through in black pencil; two blue pencil strokes in left margin.
174 Entry crossed through in black pencil; one blue pencil stroke in left margin.

[*page* 122] *1762*

April 19th Granted general warrant against Jane Nelson wife of George a salt watchman in Shields for throwing bricks and stones at Francis Woodnot of ditto weaver and his daughter. sm.

20th Transferred two licenses to Edward Bennet and Thomas Bennet blacksmiths. 4s.

23rd Granted special warrant against John Comber of Gateshead shoemaker for ill treating his apprentice William Thompson. s. Agreed.

24th Took the recognizance [*inserted*, of] George Nelson of Shields watchman in £20, and Robert Barrass salt officer in £10, for the appearance of Jane Nelson at next sessions. sss4. Released.

26th Granted special warrant against Matthew Greenwell of Sunderland master for detaining £1 15s 0d wages from his apprentice John Dixon, and selling him to a man of war's crew for £16 paid in lieu of Ralph Roxby mariner, though the said John Dixon had a 3 years protection. s. *Agreed.*

27th Granted special warrant against Thomas Rawling of Whitburn labourer for defrauding J. Jefferson of Harton farmer out of £7 6s 8d under pretence of selling him a grey horse fit for drawing etc. sm. Agreed.

28th Took the examination of Richard Rogers a pauper about his settlement upon oath and request from the township of Shields. sm. Mem. Settled upon Boldon.

30th Granted special warrant against Andrew Kennings of Monk Wearmouth Shore trimmer for knocking down and *dragging* Jane Allison of ditto through a pond etc. sm. Agreed.

[*page* 123] *1762* [*8 strokes*]

May 4th Granted special warrant against Margaret wife of Thomas Dobson of Shoreside carpenter for taking of<f> a line a

linnen shift the property of Elinor Pattison wife of William skipper. sm.
N.B. This Elinor proved a perjured woman, and paid all to Mary Dobson.

Granted special warrant against John Calvery for assaulting and beating Ann Telford (both servants of Mr Todd of the Shore, shipwright) on the 3rd instant. sm. Agreed.

7th Took the recognizance of Robert Crisp of Jarro Wood farmer in £40 and William Bruce of South Heburn farmer in £20 for the appearance of Robert Crisp at the next quarter sessions. Not paid.

Granted summons warrant against Margaret Hudson of Shields wife of Benjamin Hudson mariner for 6 oaths and curses, upon the information of Ann Cockeril and Mary Gibbon. s. *Mem* She paid 6s and charges.

Granted warrant of distraint against William Grieves and others of Shields for not paying their respective rates to the poor thereof upon oath of Thomas Crawford overseer. sm. [*margin,* Mem. They paid all]

15th Granted general warrant against Isabella Brewster of [*inserted,* Sunderland] for leaving the service of Mr Samuel Stephenson of Monk Wearmouth roper. s. Awarded 10s quarter's wages, and 2s expenses.

17th Granted special warrant against James Henderson of Shields blacksmith for not paying 10s to his servant Rachel Armstrong. s. He paid the money.

18th Took the information of Margaret wife of Benjamin Hudson of Shields mariner against Mary Gibson of Shields spinster for swearing and cursing 10 oaths and curses. s. *Mem She paid 10s and charges.*

[*page* 124] *1762*

May 20th Granted special warrant against John Catron of Sunderland labourer for assaulting and beating on the breast Peter Ovington of ditto bayliff. sm. Agreed.

Granted special warrant against John Lamb of Carrs Hill miller for defrauding William Nevins of Shields labourer of 8s 6d under pretence of buying a boll of wheat for him. sm. Agreed to pay all.

27th Granted special warrant against Robert Banks junior of Monk Wearmouth shoemaker for throwing down with a rope Ann Hogget and thereby breaking her arm. s. Agreed to pay all.

June 1st Took the information of John Peper of Shields maltmaker against Mary Welton alias Blair for drunkenness this day at Shields and summoned her. s.
Mem. Mary Blair paid the money.

William Watson aged 76 labourer maketh oath that he made his last year's service about 52 years since with Mr Carr of North Biddick in the parish of Washington. o. *Note*: I hear he had an estate and voted for Sir Thomas Clavering.[175]

Elisabeth Judson of Southwick widow swore herself to be with child by Lawrence Hunter of the Cumberland Militia, taylor, and I granted warrant against him on complaint of the overseer. ssss.

2nd Sent the appointment of overseers for the poor of Hylton to Joseph Sympson and Thomas Turner, by [*blank*] Rippon a poor girl with a wooden leg, to whom I ordered the shilling. I gave orders for removing Lame Rippon her father to the workhouse and to pay him his arrears past.

[*page* 125] *1762*

June 2nd Granted general warrant against William Thompson

---

175 Under the laws of settlement, residence in a place where you owned property and paid taxes was one way to establish settlement rights. Entry crossed through in black pencil; one blue pencil stroke in left margin and one in right margin.

apprentice to John Combs of Gateshead shoemaker for leaving his master's service. s.
Agreed upon his returning to his master.[176]

4th Made the mittimus of William Millar, a stroling vagrant and deceiver for want of sureties. ss. *Note* he ran away from the constable [*name illegible*].

7th Granted general warrant against Dorothy wife of John Riddle of Shields mariner for calling Mary Taylor [*inserted*, wife of Ralph mariner] a witch and threatening her life. sm. Agreed at 5s. N.B. They are both scolds and fools.

Granted special warrant against Ann Holyday of Shields milk-seller for refusing to sell [*blank*] Barkas of Hartons Mill according to the wages agreed on. ss.

9th Granted general warrant against Thomas Peele, Edward Fletcher, Edward Rogers, William Rogers and Joseph Johnson [*inserted*, pitmen], for leaving the work of J. Blacket Esq. at Heworth Colliery. sm. Agreed and the men paid the expenses.

10th Took the recognizance of Joseph Yellowly of Hylton farmer in the penalty of £10 and Joseph Yellowly of ditto farmer in £5 for the appearance of the said Joseph at the quarter sessions. sssm. [*margin*, Mr Hutton's warrant][177]

10th Elisabeth Marshall of North Biddick, Washington [*inserted*, single woman] swore her self to be with child by John Brown of Chaters heugh in Chester-le-Street parish, wright, and I granted my warrant against him on complaint on Richard Whin. sms.
N.B. She was tryed for a larceny in 1760 and acquitted.[178]

12th Granted special warrant against George Forrest of Shields saltmaker for assaulting, bruising, threatening, and breaking the

---

176 Entry crossed through in black pencil; two blue and two black pencil strokes in left margin.

177 Yellowly was fined 6d: DRO, Q/S/OB 12, p. 142.

178 An Elizabeth Marshall, spinster of Norton, was branded for theft from a house (e.g. found guilty of a lesser charge, of grand larceny) at the assizes of 1761: PRO, DURH 16/1. There is no record of her at the quarter sessions.

windows of Mr John Hill of Westo his master on the 5th instant. sm.

[*page* 126] *1762* [*1 stroke*]

June 14th Granted special warrant against George Smith servant to Francis Thompson of the Shoreside innholder for beating Edward Hardy a boy and his fellow servant. s. *Note* the master turned him away.

Granted special warrant against John Jackson of Shields apprentice to a boat-builder for kicking Sarah Davison servant to [*blank*] Fryar the barber, and threatening farther mischief. sm. Agreed.

17th Granted general warrant against Andrew Cannon, John Snowden, Christopher Lamb, George Anderson and Joseph Atkinson all of Monk Wearmouth Shore labourers for leaving the service of John Usher of ditto ballast-master. sm.

Committed them all to the House of Correction for one kalendar month. 2 sm. Superseded.

Granted general warrant against John Jackson officer of the customs in Shields for refusing to pay 10s wages to Barbara Ridley of ditto. o. *Note* he paid her and constable.

22nd Granted special warrant against Thomas Richardson of Shields blacksmith for assaulting and bruising Mary Wilkinson of ditto. sm.
Agreed.

24th Removed Mary Dryden widow of Thomas Dryden with Thomas and Michael Dryden, children of the said Mary and Thomas of Monk Wearmouth, mariner, from Shields to Monk Wearmouth. sss.

26th Granted special warrant against William Jefferson of Shields keelman for assaulting and bruising James Moore of Shields skipper. sm. Agreed.

Made a mittimus for John Catron upon his not finding bail for his good behaviour. ss.
[to right *Superseded*]
Note Mr George Harrison undertook to make up the matter.

[*page* 127] *1762*

June 29th Granted general warrant against Catherine wife of George Dennem of Monk Wearmouth Shore ropeseller for beating and threatening Hannah Robinson of ditto. sm.

Granted summons warrant against John Younghusband of Shields salter for turning away Jane Lofthouse from his service before the expiration of her year. o.
N.B. She had the foul distemper.

30th Committed the above Catherine Dennam for want of sureties and upon her husband's letter. ss.

Isable Scot of Monk Wearmouth Shore [*inserted*, single woman] swore her self to be with child by John Calberry, alias Calvery, clerk to Mr William Todd shipbuilder of Monk Wearmouth, and I granted my warrant against him, on complaint of the overseer Andrew Brown. sms.

July 5th Granted special warrant against Paul Harrison of Staithe<s> in Yorkshire mariner for giving no victuals to, and refusing to pay, his apprentice Robert Clarke of Monk Wearmouth *millwright* [*inserted*, of] 2 guineas. s.

16th Granted general warrant against Francis Smith widow breadseller of Shields for assaulting etc. Elisabeth Thompson of ditto widow. sm. Dismissed.

Granted special warrant against Mary wife of Francis Howe of Monk Wearmouth aleseller for throwing water upon and throwing down Thomasine Patterson of ditto. sm. Agreed.

Granted special warrant against Elisabeth wife of George Gilchrist of Shields labourer for charging Margaret Richardson with stealing an apron, and ordering her to enter into recognizance for proof thereof. s. Agreed upon paying charges, and denying she said so.

[*page* 128] *1762*

July 17th Removed Dorothy Johnson wife of Christopher Johnson soldier in General Lambton's Regiment together with Joseph and 2 other infants from North Biddick in Washington parish to Harraton and Fatfield township in Chester parish and took the information of Anthony Richardson for that purpose. sss.

Granted special warrant against Ann Moor and Sarah Cousins of Shields for bruising Jane and Mary Moor of ditto. sm. Agreed.

Granted special summons warrant against Thomas Clarke of Symey Side[179] for not paying Isable Rutter of Shields milkseller. s. Agreed on Clarke paying 5s.

Granted special warrant against Anthony Cousins of Shields, boatman for beating and threatening Margaret wife of Robert Wood of ditto labourer. sm. *Mittimus on the 19th.* ss.

Granted peace warrant against Mary wife of William Morrison of Shields mariner and Elisabeth Hord spinster for meeting with apronfull of stones and brickbats John Paul of ditto mariner. sm. Agreed.

19th Granted general warrant against Mary Hayton of Monk Wearmouth [*inserted*, wife of John Hayton keelman] for throwing down, beating, and threatening Jane Lawson of ditto. sm. Mem. Made her mittimus. ss.

Margaret Hutchinson of Whitburn single woman swore herself with child by William Potts of Sunderland cabinet maker from Candlemass week. N.B. He gave security I hear.

Removed Margaret Hutchinson from Whitburn to the Shoreside, upon her affidavit. sss.

---

179 I.e. Simonside.

Made mittimus to Durham Gaol for Anthony Cousins. s. [*margin*, Superseded]

20th Granted general warrant against Theophilus [*inserted*, Noble] of Sunderland pilot for making a riot and breaking the windows of his father Robert Byars of ditto tylemaker. sm.

[*page* 129] *1762*

July 21st Committed Theophilus Noble to Durham Gaol for want of sureties. ss.

Granted warrant against Ann Rogers and Alice Murray of Monk Wearmouth for being persons of ill fame and attending in the bawdry house of Ann Coarser at the Shoreside. sm.

Committed Ann Coarser of the Shoreside to the House of Correction for keeping a disorderly or bawdry house there, and not finding sureties. ss.[180]

Bound over Martin Robinson constable there in £30 and Joseph Bright [*inserted*, writer] overseer, Thomas Holborn butcher, and George Sparke housekeeper [*inserted*, in £10 each] there to prosecute the said Ann Coarser. sssm.

22nd Granted general warrant against George Hopper of Sunderland boatbuilder for cruelly kicking and laming his apprentice Henry Dixon. s.[181]

24th Bound over George Hopper in £20 to appear at the next general quarter sessions at Durham for the above offence. o.[182]

Granted general warrant against Jane wife of George Dixon of Birtley waggoner and Mary their daughter for assaulting and bruising Mary wife of Thomas Potts of ditto, ditto, by throwing her over a cradle. sm.

---

180 Ann Coarser was fined 2s 6d and sentenced to one month in the house of correction; the other two were discharged for want of prosecution: DRO, Q/S/OB 12, p. 150. Edmund Tew is listed as on the bench at these sessions.

181 Three blue pencil strokes in left margin.

182 There is no record of his appearance at the quarter sessions.

27<th> Granted general warrant against Stephen Carter, Robert Moody, John Scourfield, George Elliot, and Edward Elliot [*inserted*, pitmen] on oath of Joseph Elliot viewer for refusing to work, though in full health and at proper hours, in the colliery of John Blacket Esquire sm. Agreed.

[*page* 130] *1762*

July 27th Granted special warrant against Catherine Brown of Sunderland huckster for assaulting with stones and mud Margaret wife of William Blythe labourer and threatening both their lifes. sm. Agreed at 18s.

Granted peace warrant against George Broom of Monk Wearmouth keelman for assaulting, beating and threatening the life of Elisabeth wife of Richard Broom of ditto alehouse keeper. sm.

28th Bound over George Broom in £20, and Richard Broom in £10 for the appearance of George Broom at the next quarter sessions. sss4. Superseded. o.[183]

Made Catherine Brown's mittimus to the workhouse at Durham for want of sureties. ss. N.B. Mr Wharto<n> took bail for her.[184]

Granted general warrant against John Sim of Shields for refusing to work for his master Alexander Morrison of ditto brickmaker to Mr Fairless. s. Agreed.

30th Ordered the overseers of Heworth to relieve Elisabeth Gatis and 5 infants, or to show cause before me. s.

31st Removed Elisabeth Gatis widow, together with Ann, Elisabeth Mary and Sarah children of George Gatis and the said Elisabeth from Heworth to Gateshead. ss.

183 There is no record of his appearance at the quarter sessions.

184 Richard Wharton, an active magistrate who was mayor of Durham; he was also notorious for having challenged Sir Robert Eden to a duel in 1753, but this seemingly did no damage to his career on the bench: DRO, Q/S/OB 11, p. 54.

Granted general warrant against John Robson and George Brett near Gisborough in Yorkshire kelp-merchants, now of Whitburn, for detaining £2 10s 0d from Jane Davison of Whitburn aforesaid. ss.
Mem. I settled the account at £2 3s 6d and saw the money paid.

August 4th Granted special warrant against John Richardson of Pipewell Gate, in Gateshead, for bruising and threatening Philip Usher of Felling Shore cinder-burner. sm.

[*page* 131] *1762*

August 4th Granted special warrant against Frances Brown wife of Ralph, salter, for beating and t<e>aring the cap of Ann Luckey of ditto. sm.

5th Made Frances Brown's mittimus to goal. o.

Released Theophilus Noble from goal upon his father Robert Byars releasing him from security of the good behaviour. ss.

6th Granted special warrant against Michael Joplin of Offerton keelman for taking away the good name and fame and besetting the house in the night time of Catherine Waugh of ditto widow. sm. Agreed, but *Catherine Waugh* is a bad woman.[185]

24th Granted another warrant for apprehending William Potts of Sunderland cabinet<maker> for getting with child Margaret Hutchinson of the Shoreside. sm.

Hannah Wood of Shields singlewoman swore her self to be with child from about the middle of February by James Black of ditto mariner, and I granted my warrant against him. sss.

26th Margery Dixon swore her self to be with child from after Christmas 1762, and that Ralph Young mariner is the father of it. s. Dead born.

September 1st Granted special warrant against Mary Anthony

185 Entry crossed through in black pencil.

widow, for throwing bricks and threatening the life of Jane Armstrong wife of Thomas of Shields boatman. sm. Agreed.

September 6th Granted special warrant against Richard Anderson [*inserted*, pitman], and Thomas Lamb a boy of the Square Houses near Heworth for assaulting and throwing stones against Catherine Greenwell. sm. Agreed.

[*page* 132] *1762* [*5 strokes*]

September 14th Granted special warrant against Peter Wanless of Monk Wearmouth farmer for assaulting and bruising with a thick stick Christopher and Ruth Bunting on the 11th instant. sm. Agreed at £1.[186]

Granted special warrant against Esther Cousins [*inserted*, of Shields salter] for throwing large stones against the belly and head of Mary wife of George Forrest now big with child and threatening many times before to make her pick her calf, on the oath of Mary Ferguson her mother. sm. Agreed.[187]

September 6th Granted summons warrant against Sarah Cousins for leaving the service of George Forrest of Shields salter. s.
Agreed.

Granted special warrant against Mary Gibson of Shields spinster for swearing to break all the goods in the house of her brother William Gibson butcher, and threatening the life of Dorothy his wife, if she came out upon the Gallery. ss.
Agreed.

September 14th Granted special warrant against John Joplin of Monk Wearmouth skipper for endeavouring to throttle Robert Pattison of ditto skipper. sm. Agreed.[188]

---

186 Entry crossed through in black pencil; two blue pencil strokes in left margin. .

187 Entry crossed through in black pencil; two blue pencil strokes in left margin; 'her pick her calf' underlined in black pencil.

188 Entry crossed through in black pencil; two blue pencil strokes in left margin; 'throttle' underlined in blue pencil.

<1>6th Granted special warrant against James Rea, alias Reay, of Whitburn fisherman, for assaulting Edward Watson of ditto, ditto on the 11th. sm. Agreed.

Made a mittimus for Mary Gibson to the House of Correction. Superseded.

Granted special warrant against Paul Harrison mariner for beating his apprentice Robert Clark of Monk Wearmouth, and refusing him both victuals and wages <£>1. 19<s>. $11\frac{1}{2}$d, and also for threatening his life.

[*page* 133] *1762*[189]

September 18th Bound over Paul Harrison master and mariner in the sum of £20, John Wall of Sunderland fitter in £10, and Elias Thornhill of ditto ironmonger in £10, for the personal appearance of the said Paul Harrison at the next quarter sessions of the peace for the County of Durham for beating cruelly and threatening the life of Robert Clark.[190]

20<th> Granted general warrant against Alice Short of the Shoreside spinster for defrauding Edward Preston's wife of ditto butcher of 21s by giving her a false guinea for changing, for which she received an half guinea and ten shillings and sixpence. sm. Agreed.

24th Granted special warrant against Thomas Oswald of Sunderland master and mariner for kicking and bruising Margaret Oswald of the Shoreside in many parts of her body. sm. Agreed.

23rd Granted special warrant against Catherine wife of William Blendenham of Sunderland taylor for bruising Agnes Gibbs of ditto, aleseller, on the 22nd. sm. Agreed.

---

189 The top 8 cm. of pp. 133–4 are cut away, but the fact that the top of the pages is dated shows this had been done before Tew started to use the page, and that no text is missing.

190 There is no record of his appearance, or of the group summoned to appear on September 28th.

[*page* 134] *1762*

September 27th Granted general warrant against Adam Johnson of the Shoreside mariner for cruelly beating and bruising James Cettiers a boy of 9 years, son of James of ditto mariner. sm. Agreed.

28th Granted general warrant against Robert Brown of Shields saltmaker for kicking Jane wife of William Marshall, Invalid, now great with child and throwing stones etc. sm. Agreed.

Granted summons to George Partiss labourer, Barbara Anderson, Margaret Cambsby, Thomas Holborn butcher, Joseph Wallis apprentice to Pierce Hall blacksmith [*inserted*, all of Monk Wearmouth Shoreside], to appear at the next general quarter sessions of the peace at Durham. sm.

Granted general warrant against Ann Rogers and Alice Murray for frequenting the [*inserted*, bawdry] house of Ann Coarser of Monk Wearmouth now in the House of Correction. sm.

Made the mittimus for Ann Rogers and Alice Murray to the goal at Durham. ss.[191]

[*page* 135] *1762*

September 29th Granted special warrant against Ann Varey wife of Stephen Varey of Shields mason for charging Barbare Maccauly with stealing a cock chicken. sm. Agreed at 7s 6d.

30th Granted general warrant against Thomasine wife of William Donkin gardener and Frances wife of John Joplin keelman, both of Monk Wearmouth, for assaulting and threatening the life of Mr Joseph Roxby of ditto gentleman. sm. Agreed by Donkin.

Granted special warrant against Thomas and Ann Herbert of Shields ale-sellers for turning away without wages and bruising Ann Purvis. o.

---

191 This lapsed for want of prosecution: DRO, Q/S/OB 12, p. 150.

October 4th Convicted Catherine Potts wife of Thomas Potts of Shields mariner for 5 profane oaths and curses, and she paid all.

12th Wrote to Mr John Chilton of Shields alekeeper to pay the wages of his servant Alice Ward. o.

Elinor Tate of Jarro singlewoman swore her self with child by Peter Tickborn of Kello farmer. s.

13th Mary Blair, alias Welton of Shields fruiterer was this day convicted of drunkenness upon the oath of Margaret Forster of ditto and [*inserted*, would not] pay 5s to the poor, so that I ordered her into the stocks for six hours. s.

Granted special warrant against John Chilton aleseller for turning away his servant Alice Ward before the time. o.
Note he agreed to pay her for a quarter. ss. N.B. Alice Ward is an idle girl.

15th Granted special warrant against William Annesly and Thomas Deal for leaving the service of John Henzel of Shields glass maker. s.

[*page* 136] *1762*

October 15th Granted general warrant against John Sim of Shields for stealing a glass can or bottle, from Messrs Cookson and Deere. o.

Granted general warrant against Edward Cuthbertson of <*Roquer*> House for kicking and beating his servant Mary Thompson. s.
I parted them.

19th Granted special warrant against Andrew Taylor of Monk Wearmouth master and mariner for refusing to pay 10s to John Graham of ditto mariner. s. Note: he paid 10s and expenses 2s.

26th Granted general warrant against Stephen Gray of North Shields mariner belonging to the ship Industry, for getting with child Ann Brown of Sunderland singlewoman, being examined on oath. ssss.

November 2nd Removed Sarah Calendar with 5 children all infants under 9 from Shields to Cammas in the parish of Bedlington, being the settlement of the said Sarah and Alexander her husband, salter. sss.

3rd Took the information of Isable Gairnes of Shields widow against Mary Jacob aleseller for cursing 12 profane curses on the 2nd instant at Shields. s.

17th Granted special warrant against Ann wife of James Younghusband of Shields shoemaker for bruising Alice Sheriff of ditto *fruiterer*. sm.

19th Granted general warrant against James Gilleroy of Bell Key glassman for beating and bruising William Fenwick of ditto, ditto, so that he is under a surgeon's hand and cannot work. sm.

[*page* 137] *1762*

November 22nd [*inserted,* Note James Gillroy paid to William Fenwick 18s 6d for the surgeon and himself.]
Granted summons warrant for James Gillroy's witnesses. s.

Granted general warrant against James Hardy of Shields glassman for beating etc. Elisabeth wife of George Atkinson of ditto glassman. sm. Agreed at 10s 6d.

23rd Granted general warrant against Robert Hogg of Whitburn for not paying £2 12s 6d to his servant William Robson. s.
He agreed to pay.

Granted general warrant against Thomas Bruce for detaining £4 15s 0d for wages due to Michael Rochester. s. Agreed.

Granted general warrant against Robert Wallis of the Shoreside for beating and threatening Lucia Mills and her bastard son. sm.
All bad people and thiefs.

Granted general warrant against Percival Hall of the Shoreside blacksmith for detaining 10s 6d wages from Joseph Wallis. s.
Note: this is the 3rd time of his coming before me on the like account and I bound him over to the next quarter sessions under the penalty of £10. sss4. Superseded.

29th Took the information against Jane wife of James Moor of Shields lighterman for cursing six profane curses in the hearing of Elinor Scot. s.
She paid.[192]

December 2nd Granted general warrant against Sus<anna> Crow wife of Robert at the Shoreside trimmer for throwing water into the face and threatening to stab Rebecca Williamson of ditto singlewoman. sm.
Dismissed.

[*page* 138] *1762*

December 3rd Made mittimus for Mary Jacob of Shields aforementioned for refusing to pay 13s for cursing and swearing, for sixteen days hard labour. o.[193]

Granted special warrant against William Crawford of Monk Wearmouth mariner for refusing to pay 7s wages to Sarah Turner. o. Agreed.

6th Granted general warrant against John Willis of the Shore boat builder for not paying for the washing of his apprentice William Forster according to their agreement. s. Agreed.

Wrote to Mrs Shafto of the Shore boatbuilder for refusing to keep her sick apprentice. o.

9th Granted general warrant against James Davison of Monk Wearmouth labourer for beating and threatening John Gladstains clerk to Mr J. Stafford of ditto. sm. Agreed on paying 3s 6d.

---

192 Entry crossed through in black pencil; two blue pencil strokes in left margin; 'cursing six' underlined in blue pencil.

193 Two blue pencil strokes in left margin.

10th Granted general warrant Isable Wear wife of Edward saltmaker for beating and bruising Edward Cowper an infant and his grandmother Ann Nevins widow of ditto. sm.
Agreed.

13th Granted general warrant against Robert Thompson of Monk Wearmouth butcher for knocking down and bruising Jane wife of George Addison trimmer. sm. Agreed.

15th Granted general warrant against Thomas Winter of Monk Wearmouth maltman for getting with child Dinah Henderson of ditto upon her oath about the 24th June. ssss.

[*page* 139] *1762* [*2 strokes*]

December 22nd Granted special warrant against Alice Harrison of Shields salter for not coming to the service of Frances Brown of ditto salter. ss. Agreed.

Granted special warrant against Margaret Harwood of Shields salter for not coming to the service of Mary Gasket of ditto salter. ss. Agreed.

24th Granted general warrant against William Weirs apprentice to Mr Joseph Hunter of Westo master and mariner for leaving the service of his master. s.

27th Granted general warrant against several defaulters in East Boldon township for the highways upon the oath of John Forster surveyor. sm.

29th Granted general warrant against Ralph Cooper of Sunderland shoemaker for beating and bruising Grace Carter wife of Paul of ditto shoemaker threatening farther mischief. sm. Settled by Mr Mowbray.

[*page* 140] *1763*

January 3rd Granted general warrant against Jane wife of William

Morriss for beating William son of James Thompson, both of Shields and brickmakers. *Not paid.*
Note: James Thompson is a scrub rascal.[194]

10th Removed Mary Pearce alias Mackpherson (widow of the late John a Scotchman) together with their 3 children John 7 and $\frac{1}{2}$, Mary 4 and $\frac{1}{2}$, and Robert 2, from Cleadon to Cramlington in the parish of Woodhorne Northumberland, the settlement of her late father John Rutter of Cramlington, at the request of Whitburn parish. ssss.[195]

11th Granted general warrant against Elisabeth wife of George Wastal of the Shoreside mariner for feloniously taking and carrying away a cock the property of Mary Moore aleseller of ditto, on the oath of Alexander Johnson labourer. sm. Agreed.

Granted general warrant against Thomas Gibson of Cleadon farmer for feloniously taking and carrying away 4 fothers of limestones the property of James Lowes of ditto. sm.
N.B. Thomas Gibson paid all.

Granted special warrant to Peter Wanless of Monk Wearmouth farmer for £2 10s 0d wages due to his son Peter from Mrs Ann Robinson of the Shoreside widow and shopkeeper. s.

Transferred the ale licence to[196] Jane Dryden of the Shoreside to Thomas Storey keelman upon receiving a proper certificate of his behaviour. sm.

18th Granted special warrant against William Catcherside apprentice to Mr Evan Deere for leaving his work. s. [*inserted*, Not] agreed.

Granted general warrant against [*blank*] Bone of Washington labourer for stealing a cock value 2s 6d from [*blank*] Allison of ditto blacksmith. sm. [*margin*, Agreed]

---

194 Two blue and two black pencil strokes in left margin; 'a scrub rascal' underlined in blue pencil.

195 Two blue pencil strokes in left margin.

196 This should be 'from'.

[*page* 141] *1763*

January 19th Granted special warrant against Mark Brough master and mariner of Monk Wearmouth for not allowing sufficient [*inserted,* money for] victuals to his 2 apprentices Thomas and Robert Potts. o. *Note* He agreed to pay 3s per week.

22nd Granted special warrant against Joseph Elliot of Heworth agent to John Blacket Esq. for not paying the wages of Robert Salmon overman (which were paid to him by Mr Blacket) for the use of Robert Salmon, to the value of near ten pounds. ss. Agreed.

Removed Elinor wife of Joseph Justice of the chapelry of All Saints Newcastle horse breaker, and Ann their daughter aged 1 year and $\frac{1}{2}$ from the Shoreside to All Saints. sss.

24th Granted special warrant against Thomas Storey and a person called William Manners [*inserted,* now of Shields] for firing a gun [*inserted,* on] purpose to affright Christiana Mackcloudy of Harton spinster, where [*inserted,* by] the said Christiana was thrown from her horse and her elbow put out of the socket. s. Thomas Storey agreed to pay surgeon etc.

25th Granted general warrant against Andrew Young of Southwick farmer for beating and throwing into the river William Heslop of Sunderland boatman sm. Agreed at 15s 6d.

26th Granted special warrant against Ruth Bell of Monk Wearmouth innholder, for turning away from her service John Cutter. s. She paid.

31st Granted warrant against James Dick of Monk Wearmouth carpenter for striking and abusing George Longstaff senior. sm.

February 1st Made James Dick's mittimus for want of sureties. ss.

[*page* 142] *1763*

February 3rd Granted a liberate for James Dick, upon Thomas White of Durham cordwainer and John Bamborough of Sunderland bricklayer each entring into recognizance of £10 for the said James Dick's appearance at the next general quarter sessions. sm.[197]

10th Granted general warrant against James (and Frances) Thompson of Whitburn labourer for breaking windows and threatening the lifes of Jane Davison widow and her daughter. sm.

14th Granted general warrant against John Cacherside apprentice to Cookson and Deer for absenting himself from his work. sm.

April 29th Sent summons warrant against John Dickerson, alias Dixon, of Hedworth-Mill, on information of the exciseman for selling ale without license. sm.
I convicted him on his own confession. sm. And paid to Mr Railton of Jarro £1 10s 8d for the poor and 5s to the informer.

May 2nd Granted general warrant against John Crawford of Monk Wearmouth baker for knocking down and beating Alice Henderson his servant. s. Agreed.

4th Removed Elisabeth Dixon widow of James Dixon of Sunderland cordwainer deceased with 5 children from the township of Washington to Sunderland. sss.

6<th> Granted Dorothy Weddal a general warrant against her husband James Weddal for beating and bruising her with a rope, following her with a knife and refusing her a maintenance. Agreed the matter betwixt them. o.

[*page* 143] *1763* [*10 strokes*]

May 9th Granted special warrant against Henry Smith of Gateshead tallow chandler for refusing to pay 6s 6d for wages due to Joseph Haddon his servant. sm. Dismissed.

Granted special warrant against Margaret Rutter for absenting

197 James Dick or Dicks, though he occurs elsewhere in Tew's Notebook, has no recorded appearance in court.

herself from the service of Thomas Lodge of Shields brickmaker. s.

Granted search warrant against Thomas Dag of Hedworth labourer, Mary Johnson widow, and [*blank*] Arrowsmith of Gateshead Fell labourer for feloniously taking away, a bedstead, an iron spade etc. the goods of John Walker of Shields baker. sm.

12th Granted special warrant against William Morrison for leaving unfinished the work of Alexander Morrison of Shields brickmaker. s.
Agreed.

Granted special warrant against John Dickerson of Hedworth Miller for not paying £4 11s $7\frac{1}{2}$d (the price of a cloth coat, to be first deducted) for his wages. ss.

Granted special warrant against William Potts of Westo Dean-House, farmer for refusing to pay £3 2s 6d to his servant Thomas Finlay. s. Agreed.

13th Granted special warrant against Christiana [*blank*] of Horsley Hill for refusing to come to the service of [*blank*] Bowrey of ditto. s.
Agreed to come.

Granted special warrant Robert Green of Shields waterman for entering an house there, stripping himself naked and offering to fight with two women in it, and for beating and tearing the shirt of Matth<i>as Wildey constable. s. Agreed.

[*page* 144] *1763*

May 14th Granted special warrant against Ann wife of Thomas Russel of Shields master and mariner for turning away her servant Hannah Northouse and taking 14s from her box. o. Agreed betwixt them.

16th Made a mittimus for Robert Green to the House of Correction. ss. Superseded.

Granted special warrant against William Mangham and [*blank*] Lewis of Shields shoemaker for offering to carry away a goose, which they had tyed by the leg, from John Potts of Harton Moor House etc. s. Agreed at 5s.

Granted special warrant against Sarah Saburn of Monk Wearmouth Green widow for turning adrift James Doe apprentice to her late husband. s.

17th Granted general warrant against Martin Shepherd mariner, Margaret Shepherd spinster and Mary Haddock widow [*inserted*, all of Shields] for bruising with a large coal the head etc. of James Weddal mariner. sm.

Granted special warrant against Frances Thompson of Whitburn for leaving the service of George Wilson fisherman. s.

Granted special warrant against Thomas Anderson of East Boldon for turning away his maid servant [*blank*]. o. *Note* She was lazy, and he paid her 5s. o.[198]

18th Granted special warrant against Elinor Bryson for leaving the service of her mistress the wife of Lieutenant Thomas Dodd of Gateshead. s.

19th Removed William Logan, Elisabeth his wife, John, James and Margaret their children from the Shoreside to Monk Wearmouth township. sss.

23rd Allowed the license to Edward Bennet of Hedworth. sm.

[*page* 145] *1763*

May 24th Granted general warrant against Robert Farrar and John Robinson of Sunderland skippers for assaulting and bruising Robert Dodd of ditto skipper. sm. Agreed.

---

198 Entry crossed through in black pencil; two blue pencil strokes in left margin; 'Note She was lazy' underlined in blue pencil.

Granted special warrant against John Errington of Monk Wearmouth barber for beating and throwing stones against the son of Alexander Knox of ditto keelman. sm. Agreed and paid costs.

27th Granted special warrant against Ann Brown of Harton widow for lodging strolers and vagrants etc. s.[199] [*3 strokes*]

28th Granted special warrant against widow of Anthony Thompson of the Shoreside for turning away her hired servant without causes. Agreed.

30th Granted special warrant against Isable Jefferson [*inserted,* widow] and her daughter Isable for beating and bruising in divers parts of her body Jane the wife of Anthony Cousins of Shields lighterman. sm. Agreed.

Granted special warrant against Elisabeth Wilson of Shields widow for refusing to sell the milk of Mr Robert Atkinson of Jarro farmer. s.[200]

June 2nd Granted general warrant against Mary Dixon for felony (and took the information of Elisabeth Graham) in stripping her own children of shoes, stockens, 3 shifts and an happing the property of the inhabitants of Shields, and provided for the children then in the workhouse. sms.[201]

7<th> Granted general warrant by me and another justice [*inserted,* viz. Mr Carr] for apprehending William Hunter of Monk Wearmouth for getting Elisabeth Denton [*inserted,* of Washington] with child in 1760. sm.
He gave £5 to Washington parish.[202]

---

199 Entry crossed through in black pencil.

200 Entry crossed through in black pencil; two blue pencil strokes in left margin.

201 This entry presumably refers to purloining clothes provided by the parish for the poor. Entry crossed through in black pencil.

202 Although Ralph Carr was also on the bench, this is almost certainly Matthew Carr, active both at the sessions and in Sunderland, from which he ordered paupers removed, acting with Teasdale Mowbray: DRO, Q/S/OB 12, pp. 179, 254, and vol. 13, p. 45. Fathers of bastards had to pay the parish for compensation or indemnity against the costs of maintenance.

8th Granted special warrant against Mark Gardiner of Shields carpenter for refusing to pay 8s and 8d to Elisabeth Thursby his servant for wages. s.
He paid the money.

[*page* 146] *1763*

June 8th Granted general warrant against Henry Pearson of Sunderland mariner, William Love, Thomas Love, John Anderson, Thomas Purdey for bruising Matthew Fletcher of Gateshead pitman and defrauding him of 11s 6d. sm. Agreed, and paid back the money.

9th Granted general search warrant to search the house of Greg of Lamesly labourer for a webb of linnen cloth 27 yards, the property of [*blank*] Robson, farmer. ss.

10th Granted special warrant against Sus<anna> Crow wife of Robert Crow of Monk Wearmouth labourer for throwing stones and bruising Ann Short wife of Joseph wheelwright of ditto. sm.
Agreed.

13th Granted general warrant against Ann wife of Charles Higgons of Shields taylor for assaulting and threatening Mary Marsh of ditto and endeavouring to take away her good name. sm.
Agreed.

15th Granted special warrant against Lydia Sinclair for leaving the service of Elizabeth Blagdon of Shields manteau-maker. s.
Agreed.

17th Granted general warrant against a man called George Drunkey of Shields labourer for beating Lewis Ogle of ditto baker. sm.
[*margin*, Agreed]

18<th> Granted general warrant against James Moore of Monk Wearmouth mariner for striking with a pair of tongs Margaret Wheatley of ditto his servant. [*deleted*, Not paid]

20th Granted special warrant against John Coxon of Bishop Wearmouth parish alehouse keeper [*inserted*, to appear next day at ten] for refusing to pay £5 14s 0d wages to John Forbes carpenter at 7s per week according to agreement. sm.

22nd Granted special warrant against John Coxon to the said £5 14s 0d. sm N.B. He paid.

Granted special warrant against Margaret Moray wife of William of the Shore master and mariner for taking out of the box of her servant Margaret Gardner £1 11s 0d and turning her away before her time. ss. Agreed to pay all.

[*page* 147] *1763*

June 24th Granted general warrant against John Jennison of Black Fell in Chester parish for assaulting and bruising his mother-in-law Elisabeth Cowper. sm. Agreed.

Wrote to the overseer of Fatfield in Chester parish to relieve Jane Robson and 7 children. o.

25th Granted special warrant against John Hunter for leaving the service of John Steel of Harton farmer before his time. s.

28th Ordered John Hunter to pay 17s 6d to Steel and Steel paid all. ss.

29<th> Granted special warrant against Matthew Laidler foreman to William Greenwell of Monk Wearmouth ship carpenter for throwing an iron spike and stone against William Swan and bruising him. sm. Agreed upon Laidler's paying <the> charges.

Granted general warrant against William Hindson and George Graham of Lamesly pitmen for breaking into the house by lifting the door of<f> the crooks of Mary Newton of ditto widow and bruising her private parts with his (William Hindson's) fingers, and also for both of them throwing [*inserted*, several times] on

the ground Ann Stringer wife of John of ditto pitman on Sunday past ten at night. o.
N.B. They agreed to pay the woman a guinea.[203]

Granted general warrant against Nicholas White and Robert Hardy of Gateshead mariners for tearing the wastcoat and throwing on the fire Benjamin Isaac of ditto waxchandler. sm. Agreed.

30th Granted general warrant against Martin Davison of Gateshead labourer for assaulting and bruising John Gilley of ditto innholder. sm. [*margin*, Agreed]

July 2nd Granted general warrant against Ralph Hylton of Monk Wearmouth mariner for assaulting and threatening Elisabeth Dobson of ditto widow. sm. Agreed.

4th Granted special warrant against Robert Maccauley of Shields shoemaker for not learning his trade to Robert Lazel. s. Agreed to give indentures.[204]

[*page* 148] *1763* [*10 strokes*]

July 6th Granted special warrant against Anthony Cousin, Ralph Butimen and William Hall of Shields keelmen, for neglecting the service of Mr William Thompson of ditto mercer. o.

8th Granted special warrant against Thomas Huntley of Chester tallow chandler <for> not paying £2 11s 10d to William Umfreville for wages. s.

Granted special warrant against 5 of Hedworth for not performing a peice of mowing for J. Wilson butcher of Shields. Agreed.

11th Sent to overseer of Gateshead to allow William Reed and

203 Entry crossed through in black pencil; two blue pencil strokes in left margin and two in right margin.
204 To give up or surrender the indentures meant to cancel the apprenticeship.

wife 1s 6d per week, till they remove them to Jarroe, or to show cause at 4 to morrow afternoon. o.

Summoned Henry Richardson of East Boldon to appear at Peter Blenkinson's on the 14th for neglecting his six days highway work in 1762. o. Agreed to work 12 days this year 1763.

12th Took the oath of John Gilley constable, that he served the above summons warrant upon Thomas Hunter at Chester-le-Street. s.
Took the oath also of William Umfreville of the debts.

Granted special warrant against the said Thomas Hunter for payment of the above £2 11s 10d. sm.

15th Granted warrant against Joseph Patterson of Shields for putting out the right eye of [*blank*] Robson an infant of 6 years.

18th Granted general warrant against Mary Hall of Sunderland single woman for assaulting and bruising Mary Swinburn of Monk Wearmouth washerwoman. sm.

Granted general warrant against John Dixon of Bell-Key taylor for not paying Robert Atcheson his wages 10s 9d. Agreed.

[*page* 149] *1763*

July 19th Granted special warrant to Thomas White of Whickham waggon-wright for refusing to learn his trade to his apprentice Thomas Woodcock. s. [*margin,* Agreed]

21st Took the information of Thomas Oliver of Lamesly innholder against Jane Thompson of ditto widow for selling ale without a licence. sm.
N.B. Peter Scorer [*inserted,* of Shield Row in Tanfield] is her brewer that serves her.

25th Granted special warrant against Margery Brown saltmaker for refusing to work according to agreement with Robert Gascoign of Shields saltmaker. s. Agreed at present, being ill.

26th Granted general warrant against Mary wife of George Clark of Ravensworth-Township pitman for assaulting [*inserted,* etc.] Thomas Smith of ditto. sm.

August 1st Granted special warrant against John Crawford of the Shore for turning away Joseph Chicken before the term of his service. s. Agreed.

Granted general warrant against Mary Hills for absenting herself from the service of Joseph Sympson of Hylton farmer. sm. Agreed at 8s.

2nd Removed Jane Robson [*inserted,* widow] and 7 children from Harraton to Washington. ssss.

Granted general warrant against Hannah Menham wife of Thomas Menham glassmaker for assaulting Isabella Lowerson of Shields midwife. sm. Agreed.

3rd Granted special warrant against Thomas Akenhead and Robert Wood of Shields tylemakers for absenting themselves from Mr J. Hill's service 2 days. s.

4th Committed the said two persons to the House of Correction. ss.
Superseded.

5th Took the information and oath of Henry Gray of Shields labourer that he had lost £9 3s 0d, and granted special warrant against William Got [*inserted,* roper] and his wife for taking the said money out of his box left by him to their care. sm. Cleared, by their oaths.

[*page* 150] *1763*

August 6th William Got and his wife both took their oaths, that they knew nothing of William Gray's £9 3s 0d. o.

8th Granted general warrant against the said William Got upon his having bought a watch, buckles etc. for felony. o.

10th Wrote to Mr Thomas Millrose master and mariner about stopping his servant [*inserted,* Margaret Gardener's] wages. o. Agreed to pay 12s 6d.

15th Granted special warrant against Robert Stewart for assaulting, beating and threatening Robert Cousin, both fishermen of Shields. Agreed.

18th Granted special warrant against Benjamin Philips of Jarro labourer for taking a field to mow (and leaving it half done) the field of Thomas Carr butcher. s. [*margin,* Agreed]

20th Granted general warrant against Thomas Atkinson of Shields master and mariner for assaulting and threatening the life of John Bruce of ditto weaver. sm.

Granted special warrant against the same for ill treating and threatening the life of his apprentice Thomas Bruce. s.

Granted special warrant against Margaret Roxby of the Shoreside alehouse-keeper for detaining the wages £2 due to Ann Maddison. s.
Agreed to pay.

Granted general warrant against Thomas Fairgrave of the Shore, glazier, for assaulting and kicking Mary wife of William Laidler of the same. sm. Agreed at 8s 6d.

22nd Granted special warrant against Joseph Fackton of Shields keelman for calling Mary wife of Robert Smith of ditto keelman a whore, and breaking thereby the peace betwixt her and her husband. sm.[205] [*margin,* Agreed]

Granted general warrant against George Crawford of Shields glassmaker for beating and bruising Elisabeth Heaton of ditto widow. sm. Agreed.

205 Entry crossed through in black pencil; three blue pencil strokes in left margin.

[*page* 151] *1763*

August 22nd
Bound over Thomas Atkinson master and mariner in £20 and John Bruce of Shields weaver and his witness in £10 each to prosecute the said Thomas Atkinson at the next quarter sessions. o. Superseded.

23rd Granted special warrant against Edward Grey of Shields joiner for terrifying and threatening Elinor Mitford of ditto widow to burn and take away her life. sm. Agreed.

24th Granted general warrant against Isable Reed of Shields singlewoman for assaulting and throwing water against Ann Graham aleseller of the same. sm. Agreed to pay 6d per week.

26th Convicted Edward and Margaret Watson of Shields saltmakers for drunkenness and gave out warrant to the churchwardens of Shields to receive 10s.

Jane Rames of Shields single woman swore a bastard child, [*inserted,* from about Lady day last] to William Young of ditto glazier and I granted my warrant against him. sms.

27th Granted general warrant against Ann Brown of Shields saltmaker for assaulting and threatening to fire the house of her brother William Brown of ditto. sm.

29th Granted special warrant against Nicholas Crofton of Follingsby farmer for assaulting and striking William Smith of Monk Wearmouth farmer. sm.

Granted special warrant against Elisabeth and Jane Addison for refusing to work at 1s per day with the said William Smith, according to agreement. s. Agreed, upon their returning to work and paying charges.

Bound over Nicholas Crofton of Follingsby to the next quarter sessions under the penalty of £10-0s. Superseded. o.

[*page* 152] *1763*

August 30th Granted general warrant against Margaret wife of William Feaster of Monk Wearmouth keelman for bruising Isable wife of William Maxfield of ditto blacksmith. sm. Agreed for the charges.

Granted general warrant against James Hall of Monk Wearmouth master and mariner for inhumanly beating Peter Covey of ditto mariner. sm.
Agreed at 10s 6d and paying the surgeon.

September 5th Granted special warrant against William Millender of Shields labourer for not coming to his work according to agreement with William Yellowly of North Pastures, farmer. ss.

Granted general warrant against William Milburn of Newcastle plumber for knocking down and cruelly beating near Sarssons gate, on the 20th August, Matthew and Jane James. sm.

7th Ordered Edward and Jane Watson saltmakers into the stocks for 6 hours. o.

Granted special warrant against James Moray of Shields for leaving the service of his master J. Anderson. s.

Granted special warrant against Robert Lumley of Shields master and mariner for assaulting, beating and threatening Matthew Wilson of ditto labourer. sm.

10th Granted general warrant against Jane Atkinson [*inserted*, widow] for assaulting etc. James and Ann Younghusband cobler (all of Shields) two days together. sm.

13th Granted general warrant against Alice Kirby of Shields widow and aleseller (and Margaret Adamson her servant) for feloniously stealing and carrying away above £145 in money, the property of her own father John Haslop, late butcher there, concerning which I took his information on oath. sms.

23rd Granted special warrant against Thomas Storey for leaving the service of Mr George Smith of Shields shipbuilder. s.

[*page* 153] *1763* [*2 strokes*]

September 24th Granted general warrant against George Humble of Birtley gentleman for not paying £6 13s 1d to Thomas Cockburn and Gilbert labourers due to them for wages. sm.

26th Granted special warrant against George Smith of Southwick labourer for threatening etc. Joseph Harrison of ditto. s.

Took the information of William Gibson of Shields butcher that Thomas Glover butcher swore and cursed 20 profane oaths and curses at Shields on the 24th. s.

27th Granted general warrant against James Wardel of Shields boatman for driving spikes into the chamber of Alexander Gray of ditto labourer etc. sm.

Granted general warrant against John Elltringham of Hallingside in Whickham parish farmer for detaining 8s 8d wages due to William Hunter (James Cragg's servant) of West Boldon. o.

28th Granted general warrant against Thomas Baines of the Shoreside joyner for assaulting, beating and threatening Isable Gilchrist. sm.

October 4th Granted general warrant against Elisabeth Punshon widow of the Shoreside for conveying out of the house of her son-in-law Ephraim Pattison of the same mariner, a bed and bedding and curtains, 6 teaspoons and tongs, a webb of cloth and 4 gowns of his late wife. sm.

7th Summoned Mary, alias Robt,[206] Cleghorn to enter into recognizance to prosecute Ann Marley whom she has charged with stealing £2 10s 0d out of her chest. sm. *Dropped*.

---

206 Possibly Roberta.

[*page* 154] *1763*

October 8th Granted special warrant against James Richardson of Monk Wearmouth labourer for threatening Richard Gillis of ditto sawyer so that he is afraid of his life. sm.

11th Granted a search warrant into the house etc. of William Knockles of Shields mariner on the oath of Ephraim Pattison who has lost divers cloaths and goods. o.
N.B. He found most of his goods.

11th Committed Mary Grainger servant of Mr John Rockwood of Shields master for stealing from his daughter Martha Ayre, widow and shopkeeper, ribbands, linens, cottons etc. value £4 2s 0d, upon the information on oath of the said Martha; and committed also Jane wife of William Ma<u>gham of ditto shoemaker, for receiving such stolen goods, knowing them to be so, several of which were found in her house, and in the houses of Thomas Richardson and Mary Taylor of ditto to whom Jane had sold them. Bound over Martha Ayre to prosecute, and Thomas Crawford, [*blank*] Young, [*blank*] and Gilbert Purvis constables as witnesses, in the penalty of £10 each. sm. sm.[207]

12th Committed Thomas Glover to the House of Correction for swearing and cursing. ss. Superseded.

14th Granted general warrant against George (called George Hall) of Monk Wearmouth weaver for assaulting etc. Dorothy wife of [*blank*] Laverick of ditto mariner. sm.

Granted special warrant against William Mackenzye of Shields taylor for threatening etc. George Hog of ditto taylor. sm.

17th Granted search warrant into the houses of of [sic] Arthur Hoadley and Martin Wanless of High Heworth labourers. o.

---

207 Mary Grainger pleaded guilty and was branded for grand larceny, assizes 1764. Jane Maugham or Mangham was transported for fourteen years: PRO, DURH 16/1.

[*page* 155] *1763* [*1 stroke*]

October 17th Granted general warrant against Martin Wanless a boy and Arthur Ottley or Hoadley (being present) both of High Heworth for stealing of<f> an hedge a shirt and shift belonging to L. Grey's servants. s.

18th Committed Margaret wife of Ralph Wanless to the House of Correction for encouraging and receiving goods stolen by her said son Martin and concealing Arthur Hoadley alias Ottley charged with felony. o.
[*margin*, Superseded][208]

19th Granted search warrant of the house of John Black farmer and of Hendon Mill and house for goods thrown by the wreck of the Industry of Shields and thrown on the shore and some of them carryed into the above houses. o.

Granted special warrant against Thomas Elliot of Whitburn farmer for defrauding and carrying away by night 17 carts of stone from the heap of Elisabeth Purviss widow. s.
Agreed to pay 18s by the 3rd November.

Granted general warrant against Henry White of the Constant John, master, for refusing to pay 10<s> 6<d> to John Laveric and the crew for wages for [*inserted*, their] delivering at a 2nd port. s.

Granted general warrant against John Crawford of the Shore baker for not paying £3 wages to John Gray and £1 10s to another servant. s.

20th Granted general warrant against Thomas Townbull of the Shoreside shipbuilder for getting with child Amy Hunter who swore against him. sms. *Mem* Renewed the warrant upon his running away. sm.

---

208 Margaret Wanless (or Wandless) was tried, for theft, and sentenced to transportation for seven years: DRO, Q/S/OB 12, p. 218, 11 January 1764. She had a child in jail, which the county treasurer found expensive: DRO, Q/S/OB 13, p. 108, 19 January 1767.

Mem. Robert Whinny of High Felling farmer and Robert Hall of Elswick LP[209] farmer entered into recognisance £10 each for Margaret Wanless's appearance next quarter sessions 3s 4d. Cancelled on her commitment.

[*page* 156] *1763*

October 21st Granted general warrant against James Coldwell barber of North Shields for assaulting and beating under the breast Sarah wife of William Kirton of North Shields apothecary at South Shields on the 19th instant. sm. A vile perjury.

Committed Jane wife of Arthur Ottley of High Felling in Jarro to gaol on suspicion of felony. s.[210]

24th Granted general warrant against John Gillroy for leaving the service of Jacob Wilson at Bell Key. s. Agreed.

29th Granted general warrant against James Weddal of Shields boatman for beating, and chaining down to a log for more than two hours, Dorothy his wife, when naked, and threatening her life etc. sm. Gone into the King's service.[211]

31st Granted summons against Margaret Johnson of Suddic[212] for charging Alice wife of Benjamin Taylor of ditto labourer with stealing a rye loaf. s. Agreed.

Committed James Weddal of Shields boatman to the House of Correction, till he find sureties. Mem. I consented that he [*verb illegible*] into the Navy.

Granted general warrant against [*blank*] Wood apprentice to William Blacklock of Shields bricklayer for refusing to work. s. Agreed.

---

209 I.e. Lordship.

210 Jane Ottley was convicted of petty larceny and transported for seven years: DRO, Q/S/OB 12, pp. 218–19, 11 January 1764, and p. 264.

211 Entry crossed through in black pencil; four blue pencil strokes in left margin.

212 I.e. Southwick.

November 1st Granted general warrant against Hannah Rippon of Shields spinster for burning the face of John Rutter. s. [*inserted*, Mem Not bound over]

5th Granted general warrant against James Moore of the Shore aleseller for bruising his servant Sarah Stoddard and not paying 4s due to her for wages. o. He paid.

[*page* 157] *1763*

November 7th Dorothy Bramwell of Outside Hall in Chester swore a female bastard child born 23rd September last to Robert Wade [*inserted*, junior] of Fatfield House farmer before J. Fenwick Esq. and me, and we thereupon issued our warrant. sms.
N.B. The above woman had sworn it before to another, so the township dropped it on payment of 3 guineas.

Granted special warrant against John Harrison of Sunderland carpenter for beating and bruising John Dodd of the Shore keelman on the 5th instant. sm. Agreed.

8th Bound over (on Mr Hutton's warrant) Joseph Topcliff master and mariner in £10, Richard Walsh alehousekeeper and William Nicholson in £5 each to the next quarter sessions. sss. Agreed. ss.[213]

11th Bound over the above Robert Wade farmer in £20 and John Wylam in £10 farmer to the next quarter sessions at Durham. sss. [*blank*]. Both of Harraton near Chester.
Dropped. ss.

14th Granted general warrant against Robert Ingram and [*deleted*, Robert] Joseph Parker apprentices to William Greenwell of the Shore, ship-carpenter, for leaving their services. s. Agreed.

Took the information of Elinor Rogers against Elisabeth Robinson of the Square Houses for stealing a table cloth and pillow slip,

---

213 In 1765 Joseph Topcliff was convicted of contempt for not being willing to serve as overseer of the poor of Monkwearmouth, and fined 1s: DRO, Q/S/OB 12, p. 278.

value 4s 6d, and bound over Elinor Rogers and William Wynne to prosecute in £5 each. sm.
Made also the mittimus of the said Elisabeth Robinson to the House of Correction. Superseded. Not agreed.[214]

Took the bail of John Robinson in £10, James Jefferson in £5, and James Chism in £5, all pitmen and of Jarro parish for the above Elisabeth Robinson at quarter sessions next. sss.

[*page* 158] *1763*

November 15th Granted general warrant against Isable Reed [*inserted,* of Shields fruiterer] for defrauding [*blank*] of ditto widow of a pair of shoes. sm. Agreed.

18th Elisabeth Saunderson of Southwick [*inserted,* spinster] swore a child against Edward Browel of Monk Wearmouth master and mariner and I granted general warrant against him. sss. She dyed and the child dyed.

22nd Granted general search warrant against George Turner of Jarro farmer for concealing timber in his outhouses of Robert Waynman of North Shields. sm.
Agreed.

25th Granted general warrant against J. Tate of Monkton farmer for detaining £1 wages from Ann and Barbara Johnson his servants. s. Agreed.

28th Granted special warrant against Michael Hunter of Bishop Wearmouth Pans mate for bruising Thomas Roxby servant of William Taylor of Monk Wearmouth on his backside against a part of the ship etc. sm.
Agreed.

December 1st Granted special warrant against [*blank*] wife of John

214 Despite her apparent release by Tew here Elisabeth Robinson was convicted and sentenced to transportation at the quarter sessions in January 1764: DRO, Q/S/OB 12, p. 218.

Hudson of the Shore barber for throwing water and striking on the arm of George Carmichael of ditto labourer. sm. Agreed.

2nd Granted special warrant against Ann wife of James Small for taking and carrying away a leathern cap from the head of Robert Cross of ditto, son of James labourer. s. Agreed.

3rd Elisabeth Vanderman of Ayres Key Bishop Wearmouth swore her self to be with child by Moses Menhem of ditto glassman, from the 5th June to 19th. s.

5th Committed Anthony Cousin of Shields skipper to the House of Correction on complaint of Mr William Thompson. sss. Superseded.

[*page* 159] *1763*

December 5th Granted general warrant against Margaret Stokoe of Shields for leaving the service of a Cullercoats fisherman. s. Agreed.

6th Granted special warrant against John Thompson carrier of the Shore for defrauding William Farmer of his sea chest etc. 12s Agreed.

Granted general warrant against John Mills of Bishop Wearmouth mariner for assaulting and threatening George Wilson of ditto skipper. sm. Agreed.

8th Granted general warrant against Michael Sutton of Sunderland master and mariner for detaining £1 3s 0d wages from John Morris. s.

Granted general warrant against Joseph Douglass of the Shore blacksmith for detaining 3s 4d wages from Alexander [*blank*] taylor. o.
Agreed.

10th Granted general warrant against [*blank*] Murray of the Shore, baker, for bruising Edward Preston on his eyes. sm. Dropped.

12th Granted general warrant against Elinor Frazier of Shields for leaving the service of Mary Moore saltmaker. s. Agreed.

19th Granted special warrant against William and John Fenwick of Bill Key bottlemakers for assaulting, beating and threatening Joseph Dickerson of ditto labourer. sm.
Agreed.

22nd Granted summons warrant against several defaulters of Monk Wearmouth Township in not working their 6 days to appear before me and Mr Fenwick at Boldon on Saturday 31st instant. o.

Granted general warrant against Hannah Gordon alias Dargue for refusing to come to work at Mr William Thompson's salt pans in Shields. s.

23rd Committed her to the House of Correction for 14 days. ss.

[*page* 160] *1763*

December 26th Signed 7 certificates for Chelsea-Pensioners. o.

26th Granted special warrant against Anthony Elstob of Sunderland mariner for assaulting and bruising James Samwell of ditto shoemaker. sm.

28th Granted special warrant against Jane Pye of Shields widow for assaulting and threatening to cleave the skull of Thomas Burdon of ditto bricklayer. sm. Dismissed.

30th Backed a warrant from Sir John Delaval against M. Graham. o.

1764

January 6th Wrote to Mr Thornberry master and mariner in behalf of Jane Bellfridge widow. o.

Signed summons warrant against Whitburn defaulters in highways. s3.

10th Granted special warrant against Joseph Wright a mariner of Bishop Wearmouth for threatening the life of his wife Catherine. sm.

10th Granted special warrant against Elisabeth wife of Jonathan Wood of Sunderland carpenter for beating etc. Elisabeth Hall widow of the same. sm. Agreed.

14th Bound over Joseph Wright in £10, John Willis of Monk Wearmouth Shore boat builder in £5 and William Feaster in £5 for the said Joseph Wright's appearance at next quarter sessions. sss4.[215]

Granted special warrant against George Welch of the Shore keelman for knocking down Elisabeth his sister etc. sm. Agreed.

16th Granted special warrant against Henry Webster of Shields glassman for beating and sorely bruising Henry Moore of ditto innholder. sm.
Agreed at a guinea.

18th Dorothy Stewardson of Sunderland spinster swore a female bastard child born on her body [*inserted*, 6th December last] at Castle Eden to John Wilson of Sunderland roper. s.

[*page* 161] *1764*

Mem Bail was taken before me and J. Fenwick Esq. for Simon Longstaff [*inserted*, of the Shore] charged on suspicion of felony, mariner, Simon in £20, Robert Longstaff of Newcastle shopkeeper in £10, and Thomas Ran[*inserted*, =son] of Monk Wearmouth master in £10 for appearance at the next quarter sessions at Easter. ss. Superseded. ss.[216]

January 25th Granted special warrant against Christopher Walker of Sunderland master and mariner for taking away the good

---

215 There is no recorded appearance in court.

216 John Fenwick of Earsdon was a fellow JP and landholder in Boldon where he inherited property: DRO, Q/S/OB 12, p. 214; D/CG 8/131. He and Tew acted together on March 23rd 1764, below. There is no recorded appearance of Simon Longstaff in court.

name and fame of Susan Walker wife of Thomas carpenter saying, that she had 2 bastards and thereby breaking the peace between her and her husband. sm. Agreed.[217]

Granted general warrant against Henry Coats and Thomas Chambers of Shields fishermen for detaining 6s from William Coats their servant. s.
Note They paid him.

26th Removed Jane Millar and her son John from Whitburn to Sunderland, and signed distraint warrant on the highway defaulters in Whitburn. sm.

30th Granted special warrant against John Brown of East Boldon carpenter for assaulting etc. George Gibson. sm. Agreed at 5s.

Gave search warrant against Thomas Tinmouth, Reay etc. [*inserted*, all of Shields coble men] on oath of George Douthwait mariner lately shipwrecked for carrying of<f> his cloaths etc. o.

31st Granted special warrant against Thomas Smart of Simy Side[218] in Jarro, farmer for turning out of his house before his time John Hall his hired servant, and paying him no wages. ss. Ann Hardwick witness.

February 2nd Bound over the above Thomas Smart to the next sessions to answer the above complaint of John Hall. o.[219]

3rd Granted general warrant against the above John Hall for not coming to the service of Anthony Roxby of Hedworth. o.

[*page* 162] *1764*

February 3rd Granted special warrant against Elisabeth wife of George Atkinson of Shields glassmaker for assaulting and cutting with an iron hack Janet wife of William Millar of ditto labourer. sm. Agreed.

---

217 Entry crossed through in black pencil; two blue pencil strokes in left margin.
218 I.e. Simonside.
219 There is no recorded appearance of Thomas Smart in court.

10th Removed an infant 18 weeks old from the Shore to North Shields, the place of his birth. ss.

Granted warrant against John Wilson charged with getting with [*inserted,* a female bastard] child on Dorothy Stewardson of Sunderland singlewoman, which was born at Castle Eden 6th December last. s3.

11th Granted special warrant against William Page and George Shotton of Sunderland mariners for bruising Henry Pearson of ditto and threatening his life for assisting in pressing them. sm. Agreed.[220]

17th Granted special warrant against John Punshon of Sunderland blacksmith for feloniously stealing and carrying away a tow striped shirt from Ann Thompson of Bishop Wearmouth sempstress. sm.

Transferred a licence at Shields. sm.

20th Took the information of James Fair of the B<lue> Quarries in Jarro, against Mary Dixon widow, for keeping an alehouse there without licence. sm.
Mem. She agreed to pay at Ladyday £1 (3rd Car. 1st).

Mem I ordered a woman rogue and vagrant from Shields to be whipped by West Boldon constable and sent her back with a pass. o.[221]

20th Removed Anthony and Ann Rippon from Sunderland to Ford Lordship s3.

Took recognizance from the above John Punshon in £10, George Frame of Sunderland anchor-smith in £5, for the appearance of John Punshon at next quarter sessions on suspicion of felony. sss. Bound over Ann Thompson in £5 to prosecute.[222]

---

220 Entry crossed through in black pencil.
221 Entry crossed through in black pencil; two blue pencil strokes in left margin.
222 There is no recorded appearance of John Punshon in court.

[*page* 163] *1764* [*2 strokes*]

February 21st Ann Turner of All Saints chapelry single woman swore herself with child [*inserted,* from September last] by John Dyal of Monk Wearmouth parish near Hy[223] Bridge, servant to William Smith junior. sms.

22nd Granted special warrant against George Moor of Gateshead Fell, taylor for ill treating and threatening the life of his wife Janet. sm.
Agreed.

Margaret Storey aged above 40 of Hedworth widow swore herself with child by John Crass of ditto widower aged above 60, and I granted warrant against him. sms. He marryed her.

Wrote to the widow [*inserted,* Mary] Reed of the Key Side Newcastle, that I should be obliged to punish her 3s 4d for [*inserted,* each of the] 8½ barrels of ale sold to the unlicensed aleseller Mary Dixon. *Note* She paid £1 3s 2d.

March 2nd Granted special warrant against Isable wife of George Haft of Shields mariner for beating Ann wife of Miles Hall of ditto etc. sm. Agreed.

6th Elisabeth Fisher of Shields singlewoman swore herself with child by Thomas Brown of Whitby mariner, son of [*blank*] Brown gardener at Chirton. s.

9th Granted special warrant against James Moore of the Shore, innholder, for knocking down with an iron poker and cutting to the bone on the head Thomas Noddings of ditto, mariner. sm.

12th I this day set aside the indentures of Robert Rogerson an apprentice to the late [*blank*] Wheldon, master and mariner of Shields by consent of parents, boy and widow Wheldon. o.

---

223 Perhaps High?

14th Took recognizance from James Moore of Monk Wearmouth inholder [sic] in £20, William Nicholson of ditto shoemaker in £10, and Archibald Campbell of ditto barber in £10 for the said James Moore's appearance at Easter sessions. sss. Superseded. ss.

[*page* 164] *1764*

March 17th Granted special warrant against Walter Hunter and James Armstrong both of Sunderland taylors for sorely bruising on the face and breast Thomas Hoy of ditto taylor. sm.

Granted general warrant against Thomas Humble of Heworth Colliery for refusing to pay 12s for the wages of Thomas Smith and son. s.

19th Took recognizance of Walter Hunter and James Armstrong of Sunderland taylors, and John Taylor of ditto painter in £40 and £10, for appearance at the next quarter sessions. sss. [*blank*] Irwin innholder.

23rd Removed Mary Thompson [*inserted*, widow of Thomas Thompson] and 3 infants from Sunderland to Burnt-Moor in Houghton-le-Spring. ss.

Ditto Removed Mary Thornton widow of John, keelman, and 3 infants from Sunderland to Bishop Wearmouth. ss.

Granted general warrant from Mr Fenwick and self against William Burn of Shields mariner for assaulting Mr Joseph Hunter of Westo and Mr William Kelsey of Shields masters and mariners and threatening their lifes. s.
Agreed.

26<th> Granted general warrant against Anne Carre for leaving the service of Mr Ogle of Low Heworth. s. Agreed.

Transferred an ale licence to Mr Youens master and mariner of Shields, it being his mother's-in-law and having received a proper certificate. sm.

31st Granted special warrant against John Catron of Sunderland labourer for bruising on the face Peter Bryce of Sunderland butcher. sm.

April 2nd Committed John Catron to the house of correction upon not finding sureties. ss. Recalled.

[*page* 165] *1764* [*1 stroke*]

April 3rd Granted special warrant against James Cockburn of Shields glass-house labourer for tripping up the heels and throwing a large <brick> on the ancle of William Anderson, so that he is sorely bruised and not able to follow his calling. sm. [*margin*, Agreed]

Granted general warrant against Margaret Rowntree and [*blank*] wife of William Atkinson both of Sunderland for assaulting and threatening the lives of Peter Ovington and George Burdon barber of the same. sm. [*margin*, Agreed]

Granted search warrant into the houses of Edward Reed, [*blank*] Bowden, [*blank*] Boweron weaver, and El<ias> Smith pawnbroker, all of Sunderland for goods stolen and concealed by them, which were regularly seized by Peter Ovington aforsaid bailiff. sm.

5th Granted general warrant against Charles Carter of Sunderland barber for refusing to pay 8s 6d wages to Ann Gambsby of ditto a nurse, 1s Agreed.

6th Granted special warrant against Ann wife of Alexander Adams of Monk Wearmouth Shore weaver, for assaulting etc. Elisabeth wife of Benjamin Smith of ditto mariner etc. sm. Agreed.

Gave Richard Fawel of Heworth chapel 12s 6d for the poor of Jarro being part of £1 the widow Dixon's punishment for selling without licence.

12th Granted special warrant against Thomas Marshall of Jarro farmer for assaulting and bruising Robert Gray of ditto labourer. sm. [*margin*, Agreed]

14th Wrote to Mr Thomas Humble about paying Mr Blacket's men. o.

18th Granted special warrant against Michael Hunter of the Shore keelman for assaulting and throwing down against some timber George Smurfitt of the same keelman. sm. Agreed.

Took recognizance from Thomas Marshall farmer in £10, John Fisher exciseman of Bell Key in £5, and John Jameson of ditto in £5 potmaker, to answer Robert Grey's complaint. sss. [*margin*, Superseded]

[*page* 166] *1764* [*3 strokes*]

April 23<rd> Granted special warrant against Peter Wanless of Monk Wearmouth farmer for refusing to pay his poor assess £2 5s 0d. s. Agreed.

27th Granted special warrant against Edward Elder of Shields [*inserted*, boat builder] for turning away Ann Brown his servant without wages, being £2 10s 0d and throwing knives etc. at her and beating her.
Note: He paid the money.

30th Granted special warrant against John Smurfitt of Birtley, viewer, for spurring his horse and throwing down William Bentley of Ayton Banks pitman and greivously bruising him. sm. Summoned at the same time Abraham Dawson and Daniel Stamp of ditto witnesses.
Agreed at a guinea.[224]

May 1st Subpoen'd John Wilson, James Bradley, Thomas Cotes carpenters in the matter of Ann Thompson and John Punshon bound over on suspicion of felony. ss. Agreed.[225]

---

224 Entry crossed through in black pencil; two blue pencil strokes in left margin.
225 No indictment is known to have resulted from this accusation.

Subpoen'd ditto Ann Hardwick as a witness for John Hall servant against Mr T. [*corrected from* J] Smart. s.

5th Gave order to the overseers of the Shore to allow Thomas Armstrong and wife both sick and a child (a nurse and to pay her and) to pay weekly to them 3s per week till they shall be able to be removed to Dundee. o.

7th Granted general warrant against Margaret Henderson midwife and Elisabeth her daughter for assaulting and threatening John and Alice Clark waggon [*inserted*, wright], all of Chester. sm. Agreed.

Granted general warrant against John Pratt of the flats near Chester pitman for fraudulently taking up and carrying away £1 7s 0d peice, the property of John Holmes butcher of Fatfield. sm.

Granted special warrant against Jane Wawton of Shields singlewoman, for assaulting etc. Elisabeth Redhead of ditto aleseller. sm. [*deleted*, Not] Paid. Agreed.

[*page* 167] *1764*

June 12th Granted general warrant against Thomas a negro apprentice to John Moss, roper in Sunderland, for bruising at the Shoreside on the 10th George How mariner and drawing a knife to stab him. sm.[226]

13th Made a mittimus for the poor negro. o.

Granted general warrant against William Morris [*inserted*, labourer] for raising an uproar and breaking the windows of Thomas Thompson butcher both of Shields. sm.
He paid 6s for so doing.

Granted general warrant against John Steel of Harton farmer, for defrauding William Morris of Shields of 8s 6d on pretence of charging a guinea for him, to receive 12s 6d due to himself from

226 Entry crossed through in black pencil.

the said William Morris. sm. The money was returned and expenses paid.

Granted general warrant against Henry Elliot of Shields butcher for assaulting and bruising against the cranks of the fire Jane Anderson manteau-maker. m.
(He paid 14s like a fool as he was).

15th Granted general warrant against John Thompson of the Shoreside, Shields – carrier, John Widdifield butcher, and James Mills servant to John Thompson for assaulting, threatening, taking by the throat and offering to heave overboard Peter Blacket servant to Christopher Elliot Shields-carrier, and taking a sailor's chest away from him which he was to deliver at Shields by express order of the owner. sm.[227]

18th Granted special warrant against the wife of William Morris of Shields labourer for defrauding him of 4s 9d in selling his milk. s.
Agreed.

18th Bound over John Carlisle farmer and Matthew Robinson innholder in £5 each and John Thompson innholder in £10 for the said John Thompson to appear at the next quarter sessions at Durham.
– John Widdifield in £10 and John Carlisle and Matthew Robinson in £5 each.
– John Thompson in £10 and John Carlisle and Matthew Robinson in £5 each for James Mill's appearance.
All of them to answer the charge of assault etc. upon Peter Blacket servant to Christopher Elliot Shields – carrier. sm sm sm.
Withdrawn 6 July. 2 sss.

[*page* 168] *1764*

June 18th Granted special warrant against Elisabeth wife of Thomas Clark of Simyside[228] farmer for bruising an hired girl

227 Entry crossed through in black pencil; one blue pencil stroke in left margin.
228 I.e. Simonside.

aged 14 called Margaret Robson on her head and face against iron etc. s.
Agreed.

19th Edward Smart mason maketh oath before me that Nicholas White late occupyer of an house in the Shoreside belonging to him owes him for arrears of rent £2 6s 0d, and that he has found in the said house a leather trunk. s.
[*signed,* Ed Smart]

Granted warrant to the constable to seize the said trunk, and to break open and [*blank*] sell to the amount of £2 6s 0d and to return the overplus to Nicholas White. s.

22nd Transferred a licence to Hunter of Monkton. sm.

Granted general warrant against Andrew [*blank*] of Gateshead joyner for assaulting etc. William Smith of Hylton LP.[229] sm.

23rd Granted general warrant against Thomas Stafford of Sunderland mariner for waylaying, assaulting and wresting out of the hand of Barbara Gilchrist of ditto a guinea, which she was sent with [*inserted,* by her mistress Jane Holiday] to change and bring 12d of rales. sm. Not agreed.

[*deleted,* Granted general warrant against Thomas Stafford of Sunderland mariner for assaulting and wresting.]

Granted general warrant against Esther wife of William Wood glassman at Shields for bruising and knocking out a tooth of Elisabeth Hayton of ditto widow. sm. Agreed.

July 2nd Granted special warrant against Mary wife of Ralph Taylor of Shields mariner to enter into recognizance to appear against Jane wife of Robert Harward whom she charges with stealing 2 aprons. sm.

229 I.e. Lordship.

[*page* 169] *1764* [*7 strokes*]

July 2nd Granted general warrant against Jane Richardson of Harton servant to Thomas Barkas farmer for leaving his service. s. Agreed.

Granted special warrant against Joseph Jefferson of Whitburn Lizards for defrauding Mary Purvis of 2 chaldron of lime stones. s. Agreed and paid for.

9th Granted general warrant against Thomas Wardal of Shields butcher for refusing to learn his trade to Anthony Chilton. s.

Granted special warrant against John Stelling of Shields ship carpenter for taking away the good name and fame of Ann wife of Thomas Gibson of ditto ship carpenter and breaking the peace betwixt them. sm.

10th Granted general warrant against John Atkinson of Shields carpenter for assaulting and bruising Thomas Gibson of ditto mason. sm.

Granted general warrant against Ann Herbert aleseller at Shields for beating and endeavouring to burn with a candle her maid servant Catherine Gentle and turning her away at 11 clock at night. s.

13th Granted special warrant against Alice Taylor of Southwick wife of Benjamin for kicking on the belly Margaret Johnson of ditto wife of James and making her to miscarry. sm. Agreed for the charges.

Committed the said Alice [*inserted,* Taylor] for want of sureties to the county goal. ss. Superseded.

Granted general warrant against Joseph Rochester of Whitburn parish husbandman for getting with child Mary Pood of ditto single woman. sms. Note: He marryed her.

16th Granted general warrant against Barbara Dunn alias Storey of Shields spinner for rifling the chest of George Haswell brick-maker. s. Agreed.

Granted special warrant against John Williamson [*inserted*, son of Jane Dawson] of Ayton Banks mariner on suspicion of stealing a £3 12s 0d the property of John and Jane Dawson of ditto and threatening both their lifes. s. Agreed.

Transferred Francis Thompson's licence at the Shore to John Thompson. sm.

[*page* 170] *1764*

July 21st Granted special warrant against Jane Maxfield of Monk Wearmouth spinster for robbing the shop of Onesipherous Dagnia of ditto shopkeeper of a roll of striped [*inserted*, ribband] and 4s 2d. sm.[230]

24th Committed the said Jane Maxfield to the house of correction. ss.

25th Granted special warrant against Robert Dixon of Shields mariner, for bruising and threatening Joseph Forster another mariner of his ship. sm.

Granted general warrant against Michael Hunter of the Shoreside aleseller for assaulting and bruising William Feaster, throwing him over the Key, and bruising the said Elisabeth etc. sm.

27th Bound over Robert Dixon in £10 and Thomas Harrison master and mariner in £5 for Robert Dixon's appearance. ss.

Granted general warrant against James Moore apprentice to [*blank*] Wedderburn of Shields blacksmith for leaving his master's service. s. Agreed.

---

230 Jane Maxfield or Maxwell was whipped for petty larceny, DRO, Q/S/OB 12, p. 264. Dagnia was one of the younger sons of John Dagnia of South Shields, gentleman, one-time owner of a Cleadon estate: Surtees, *History and Antiquities*, vol. 2, p. 55.

Granted general warrant against Jane Pye of Sheilds widow for stealing coals from John Henzell of ditto glassmaker etc. sm.

30th Wrote to Richard Wynn of Great Usworth about his servant wanting victuals. o.

Granted general warrant against William Carr of Gateshead Fell pitman for fraudulently detaining a silver watch borrowed of his brother James. sm. Agreed.

Granted general warrant against Ann the wife of James Henderson of Shields blacksmith for offering to stab Thomas Conyers of Chester, bayliff, if he seized on her goods. sm. Agreed.[231]

Bound over Jane Pye in £10, Thomas Burn wheelwright of Shields in £5, and William Pye of Houghton Pans Northumberland in £5. sss. Released.

31st Made the mittimus for Michael Hunter. o.

Took the informations of Mary wife of George Reed of Gateshead labourer and milkseller, and of Elisabeth Trumball of the Long Stairs in Newcastle against Mary Thompson of Gateshead single woman for stealing cap, knot, and bucles the property of the said Mary Read, and committed the said Mary Thompson to goal.[232]

[*page* 171] *1764*

August 1st Bound over Michael Hunter in £10, William Greenwell in £5, and James Hall trimmer in £5 for Michael Hunter's appearance. smm.[233]

6th Granted general warrant against Robert Wood apprentice for leaving the service of his master William Blacklock of Shields mason. s. Agreed.

8th Granted general warrant against Mary Cock of Shields widow

231 Entry crossed through in lack pencil.
232 She was acquitted of grand larceny, assizes 1764: PRO, DURH 16/1.
233 There is no recorded appearance in court.

for threatening and throwing water on Deborah Watson of ditto widow. sm. Agreed at 7s 6d.

Granted general warrant against Martin Gray and James Potts of Gateshead pitmen for ravishing Elinor Carruthers of Rothbury singlewoman aged 17 in a field near Gateshead etc. sm.

Note: This Elinor Carruthers was proved to be a *common strumpet*.

13th Committed William Lorrain apprentice to Mr Thomas Winship of Shields shipwright for refusing the lawfull commands of his master to pump at his dock (for 3 weeks). sss.

Granted general warrant against Patrick Wilson of Shields brickmaker for threatening the life of Alexander Morrison of ditto brickmaker. sm.

20th Granted general warrant George Reay of Shields cobleman for beating Joyce Wilkie widow, and Elisabeth Wilkie, and threatening their lifes etc. sm.

Transferred an ale licence at Monk Wearmouth to William Fleming. sm.

Granted special warrant against [*blank*] Mapes, mariner for stealing a silk hat a blanket, etc. of Elisabeth Walker of Shoreside spinster. s.

Granted general warrant against Thomas Atkinson of Cleadon for getting with child Alice Pennyman of Shields single woman, on the request of H. Ridley overseer. sm.

24th Granted special warrant against Ann wife of William Redforth of Sunderland labourer for beating etc. Elisabeth wife of J. Telford of ditto labourer. sm.

27<th> Isable Muscles [*inserted*, of the Shoreside washer woman] swore herself with child by Henry Frogging or Foggat mariner of Monk Wearmouth, and I granted my warrant against him. sms.

[*page* 172] *1764*

August 28th John Henzel desired to release recognizance against Jane Pye etc. ss.

29th Committed Ann Redforth wife of William, a porter in Sunderland to the house of correction for want of *sureties*. ss.

September 4th Granted general warrant against Sarah Calendar of Shields saltmaker for bruising Jane Morriss wife of John saltmaker of ditto. sm.

Ordered the overseers of the poor to provide for Joanna Basey and [*inserted,* her] infant and to send her by sea to Dartmouth, Devonshire the place of her husband's settlement.

Granted general warrant against James Moore of Shields keelman for bruising Mary Moore, breaking 2 Delf [*i.e.* Delft] plates and threatening her life. sm. Agreed.

Granted special warrant against John Thwaits [*inserted,* junior] of Sunderland keelman for running a set-iron into the thigh of William Thompson apprentice to Francis Howe of Monk Wearmouth keelman. s. Agreed.

5th Granted general warrant against John Taylor clerk to Mr Blakiston of Sunderland and Thomas Hosmer of ditto surgeon, for bruising William Smith of Sunderland boatman and carrying of<f> his boat. sm. [*margin,* Dismissed]

13th Granted general warrant against Virtue Blenkin of Shields singlewoman for stealing £1 3s 0d and a white cap, the money and property of Thomas Fergison of ditto mariner, from Diana his wife. sm.

15th Granted general warrant against John Robson tylemaker of Shields for leaving the service of Mr John Hills.

17th Granted general warrant against John Collier of Shields shoemaker for beating and kicking Ann Cloud of Horsely Hill and defrauding her of a pair of plated buckles value 4s. sm.

21st Granted general warrant against Captain Henry Wharton for wounding with a sword the arm of Teesdale Moody, both of Bishop Wearmouth. sm.

[*inside back cover*]
The form of backing a warrant
Durham to wit Assist the bearers in executing the within warrant, in case the said [*blank*] be found within this County: Boldon.
To all constables etc. of the County of Durham.

INDEX OF PERSONAL NAMES

[- - - -] indicates a 'blank' in the notebook for the first name

INDEX OF PLACE NAMES

SUBJECT INDEX